THE CAREER CHOSE ME

The CAREER CHOSE ME

The young person's guide to choosing the right career.

Brandon Riley

XULON PRESS

Xulon Press
2301 Lucien Way #415
Maitland, FL 32751
407.339.4217
www.xulonpress.com

© 2017 by Brandon Riley

All rights reserved solely by the author. The author guarantees all contents are original and do not infringe upon the legal rights of any other person or work. No part of this book may be reproduced in any form without the permission of the author. The views expressed in this book are not necessarily those of the publisher.

Printed in the United States of America.

ISBN-13: 978-1-54561-734-2

Dedication

This book is dedicated to my parents, Kathi Stearns and Rick Riley, who believed in me to pursue my dreams!

Table of Contents

Introduction ix
Chapter 1 - Dreaming BIG 1
Chapter 2 - When you're not good at something 5
Chapter 3 - Finding your strengths 10
Chapter 4 - You're never too young 15
Chapter 5 - Pursue the impossible. 19
Chapter 6 - Pick that ONE thing 23
Chapter 7 - Show me the money 28
Chapter 8 - Going undercover 38
Chapter 9 - Invest in YOU. 43
Chapter 10 - The college dilemma 47
Chapter 11 - Do what excites you 51
Chapter 12 - Beware the robots 56
Chapter 13 - Tell your story well 60
Chapter 14 - Keep the future in mind 65
Chapter 15 - Does my personality matter? 70
Chapter 16 - Discover by example. 74
Chapter 17 - Volunteer. 80
Chapter 18 - Don't be cool 84
Chapter 19 - There are no Lone Rangers 87
Chapter 20 - Don't be afraid of the unknown 91
Chapter 21 - Say NO to things 95
Chapter 22 - The ultimate test 97

Introduction

I started thinking about my career at a very young age. I can remember dreaming about what I was going to be when I got older when I was five years old. I loved thinking about the future because, to me, the possibilities were endless.

When I was in high school, I remember thinking, *"Why is it so difficult to pick a job?"* There were so many options, variables and possibilities of failure that the chance I might pick the wrong one was really scary to me.

I could have used a book like this when I was a teenager or college student because I honestly had to figure out a lot of this on my own. Even though I was a voracious reader in high school, I didn't read many career books because, to be honest, many of them seemed rather boring, if you know what I mean.

In an effort to make this book interesting, readable, and intriguing, I've included a lot of my own stories and firsthand experiences. This is an attempt to personalize the process and show you the path I used growing up in figuring out my career. While I chose to pursue film/TV, my hope is that you will choose to pursue the career that is just right for you. This is a book for every young person who isn't 100% sure of their future career endeavors. Many of my examples and stories will speak to the film industry, however, I believe that they are generic enough that the principles can be applied to virtually any career.

I hope this book will serve as a guide to many who are wrestling with that question, *"What do I want to be when I grow up?"*

The Career Chose Me is a book about figuring out that one thing that you were made to do. When a career chooses you, you are choosing to live in a way that you are open to a myriad of possibilities that may come across your path. By putting yourself in a posture of humility you are opening yourself to more self-discovery opportunities you may have never known existed.

Use this book as a starting point for exploring the countless career opportunities you may come across. May I urge you to strongly take your time after finishing this book to fill out the review questions in the back and explore some of the links noted throughout this book.

Acknowledgements

This book could not have been written without the help of countless people over the course of my life who poured into me, mentored me, and allowed me to fail and make mistakes. I am truly grateful for the many individuals who truly cared and believed in me.

To my parents growing up, Kathi Stearns and Rick Riley, thank you both for believing in me and allowing me to pursue a difficult industry.

To my youth pastor throughout my teenage years, Kimberly Wirt, you provided me with an outlet to volunteer, serve, and discover what leadership truly means.

To my high school English and Journalism teacher, Charis Weiss, you helped me to truly understand "story" and gave me a chance to lead as the Editor of the school's Newspaper.

To my bosses and colleagues in college while working at TAMS, Kevin Roden, Brady Black, Henry Dawson, and Gloria Furman. This fabulous group of people mentored me and encouraged me to dream big.

To Joe Batluck who was an incredible example of integrity to me, thank you for showing me how to serve and lead a life that is about others.

Chapter 1

Dreaming BIG

"So many of our dreams at first seem impossible, then they seem improbable, and then, when we summon the will, they soon become inevitable."

-Christopher Reeve

I was seven years old. I remember riding in the back seat of my dad's truck with my sister. We were on our way to a concert and my dad had a friend of his attending with us. My dad's friend just happened to be Michael Ilitch Jr., the son of Michael Ilitch Sr., who was none other than the owner of Little Caesars Pizza. What was interesting about Michael Ilitch Jr. was that he did more than run the family business; he invested in films and was an executive producer. It was my first interaction with someone from the film industry and, right away, I knew that I wanted to be involved in some way. We dropped off Michael later that night and I remember telling my dad – like most seven-year-olds – that I too wanted to be a film producer. Thankfully, my dad believed in me enough to say, "That's great. You can do that."

As I write this book, I'm now thirty-four years old and am currently producing movies in Hollywood. I'm a member of the Directors Guild of America as well as the Producers Guild of America. Some days I have to pinch myself to believe that I'm really doing what I told my dad I wanted to do when I was just seven. My path to producing films didn't come easily, and was not exactly the path I expected, but I do believe that you too can do almost anything you want if you put your mind to it.

Are you dreaming big about your future and giving yourself a chance to do the impossible? Sometimes we never come close to doing the impossible because our dreams are too small.

When you are five, you believe you can do anything.

When you are ten, you believe you can almost do anything.

When you turn fifteen, you start to believe you can't do anything.

Why does that blind faith of a five-year-old not stay with us until we graduate college? Perhaps the experience of failing, getting bad grades, or not making the team was proof that maybe we can't do everything we once thought was possible. It's amazing the experience of ten years of living life can teach us what is practical and what is achievable. Part of dreaming big is being optimistic, believing in yourself, and choosing to not always listen to the voices that tell you differently. There could be a teacher, friend, or parent in your life who isn't quite sure of your dream–and that's okay. This person most likely wants the best for you . . . they may just not know how to dream big like you do. Don't let this discourage you.

Dreaming big doesn't come naturally for everyone. Some people are natural "dreamers" and others are natural "doers." I feel blessed because I tend to find myself in between both camps. I'm one who likes to do but I also like to dream.

Dreaming Big

It's possible that you have never dreamed BIG because you grew up in a low to middle income family with limited resources. Maybe the idea of earning an income more than your parents is something that is almost laughable to you. That couldn't be you.

It's possible that you have never dreamed BIG because your idea of WORK has always been a necessary evil. Your parents and your friends' parents had jobs they all hated, so the idea of having a career that you actually enjoyed would be almost impossible to fathom.

It's possible that you have never dreamed BIG because there was always that voice of doubt that said you weren't good enough or talented enough to live a life that was remarkable. You might have failed a class or gotten in trouble with the law. Maybe you're a misfit and you feel like you don't belong.

It's possible that you have never dreamed BIG because you didn't have any role models to look after. Maybe, in your opinion, everyone you know is living an ordinary life lacking in dreams and visions of the future.

It's possible that you have never dreamed BIG because you were shut down for dreaming when you were little. Maybe you told a friend or teacher your career ambitions and you were quickly laughed at.

It's possible that you have never been a dreamer because deep down you liked the idea of the safety and security of a steady paycheck. The idea of starting your own business or working freelance is so scary that it has prevented you from dreaming BIG.

These are just a sample of the many possibilities of why someone has chosen to NOT dream BIG. May I encourage you to not let any of this stop you. You cannot let your present circumstances, life experiences, or limitations keep you from dreaming BIG because you only get one life to live.

THE CAREER CHOSE ME

I remember when I was in second grade, we were sharing in class what we wanted to be when we grew up and a girl shared that she wanted to be President of the USA. I remember thinking that it was absurd to dream that BIG. Looking back, I don't know if it was that absurd to dream that big. Who knows where this girl is today. Maybe she's running for office and working as a senator. Maybe that dream to be the president propelled her to go to law school and pursue politics. Even knowing the dream may not be obtainable, the dream to do something grand was within this girl at an early age, and that is something to commend.

Dreaming BIG is something you can learn. You can start by deciding to see your life as a clean slate. Don't attach your family's economic status or your IQ level to the degree in which you can dream.

There have always been millionaires who started with nothing.

There have always been doctors, surgeons, and dentists who went into tremendous debt to finance their decade of schooling.

There have always been college dropouts and people with only a high school education who have gone on to start companies and be entrepreneurs.

There have always been people who grew up in low-income situations who went on to change their situations and now give back to their old communities.

The person who will stop you from dreaming BIG is YOU. You are the only one who can choose to dream. Your parents and friends can't dream for you. Sure, they want you to succeed, but no one will care about your future as much as YOU will. At the end of the day, it's your responsibility to determine how BIG you will dream.

Chapter 2

When you're not good at something

"The only way to do great work is to love what you do. If you haven't found it yet, keep looking. Don't settle."

-Steve Jobs

I remember when I was in third grade and people would ask me the usual question that adults ask all kids: "What do you want to be when you grow up?" I often had different answers, and quite frankly, I loved this question. I wanted to be an architect when I was five, a producer when I was seven, a meteorologist when I was ten, a journalist when I was fourteen, and an analyst for the CIA when I was seventeen. It's funny how our ideas and dreams change over time. For me, it was all about trying new things and figuring out what I was good at and what I ultimately hated.

Growing up, I remember multiple times when adults would ask me about my career ambitions. I always thought it was interesting for them to ask five-year-olds what they wanted to do when they grew up. I guess they knew the importance of starting to dream at such a young age, or maybe they wanted to be of assistance in guiding me along the sometimes dangerous road of choosing the right career. This is a powerful question to ask a kid, if you ask me. It's as if you are trusting a child to make a grown-up decision before they are potentially ready. When kids are asked this question, they are for a brief time thrown into the adult world of "real life" decision making. Kids get to put their adult hat on for two minutes and then go back to playing with dolls or Legos. It's one of the only times a kid can get excited about making adult-like decisions.

On one of those many visits to my grandparents' house when I was five, the question would arise, "So, Brandon, have you decided what you want to be when you grow up"? When I was five, the answer would mostly be that I wanted to be either a garbage man or an architect. My parents found it hysterical that I wanted to collect trash for a living, however, as a five-year-old, these guys were my heroes. They were men riding along huge trucks, taking the trash from our house each week. I'm thankful I didn't choose the route of a garbage man. I have to believe that people who end up in a career like that never had any dreams or ambitions to do something that excited them. The idea of being an architect was well received by my family because it was a career that made good money and would be in high demand. As I grew older and older, I realized that I hated drawing and I hated math. Being an architect sounded like a cool job but the more I explored what it entailed, the more I realized that doing something that sounded cool would not always turn out so well if I didn't enjoy the process.

When I was ten years old, I thought that I might be a weatherman someday. There was something that intrigued me about watching the nightly news with my parents and seeing the weatherman make predictions about the week's forecast. I was fascinated with the idea of taking scientific knowledge and predicting what

When You're Not Good At Something

weather events may occur. Later, in junior high, I decided to study meteorology as one of my science classes. I found the class to be less than exciting. I can remember thinking that if I didn't find this field of study exciting, I should definitely not pursue it as a career option. At that moment, I decided I would no longer care to pursue meteorology as a career option.

I remember watching the *Mission Impossible* movies and thinking how cool it would be to work for the CIA. I imagined myself being part of a unit that was trying to strategically take down a terrorist. This had to be the coolest job on the planet. Think about it-your job is to literally infiltrate other countries and prevent world wars. At the time, there wasn't anything more important. With all of this interest, I decided to explore this as a possible career. I knew I didn't want to be a field operative, but I did see myself planning and strategizing how to pull off the impossible. I remember looking up information on the internet about the possible education and background needed to work for the CIA. From what I could tell, computer science and programming was very important. Knowing this, I took a computer science class in high school, thinking it would be a breeze. I quickly learned that computer science did not come easy to me. Not only did I struggle with the class, I *hated* it. Not only was I horrible at computer science, I was horrible at languages and learning them. I don't know if it was the right decision at the time, but based on these two experiences I decided to give up my aspirations to be a spy and to not pursue the CIA as a viable career possibility.

It's almost like I started crossing careers off my list at a very young age. One by one I was realizing what was probably not the best career choice for me. It soon became obvious that the desire to want to pursue a certain career needed to line up with the skills that had to come with that type of job. Part of figuring out what you want to do in life is also being a bit practical in your decision-making process.

When I was in junior high and high school, I knew I wanted to make movies, but my school didn't really offer any filmmaking courses, so I decided that the next best thing for me to pursue during that time would be journalism because I would essentially be learning about storytelling and photography. Knowing this, I put all of my energy into this field of study and became the editor of the school's yearbook in junior high and later in high school became the editor of the newspaper. What was interesting about those experiences was that it really paved a path to a career that is very similar to what I am currently doing now as a producer. Back then, I was essentially managing and inspiring my peers to write and tell stories; today, I essentially do the same thing, only in a slightly different capacity.

When I was in school, I was horrible at sports, and quite frankly, I was okay with that. I knew that I didn't want to be a professional athlete and so investing a lot of time and energy into a sport just didn't make sense to me. Knowing what I DIDN'T want to be allowed me to pursue several options of what I COULD be. While most of my friends were practicing baseball, basketball, or football, after school, I was figuring out how to design a new website for the school's newspaper before Wordpress existed. I focused a lot of energy on things that I knew would benefit me many years down the road. I think the hard part about focusing on something that is in line with your career at such a young age is that oftentimes your peers aren't necessarily thinking about the future. Most of my friends who were on sports teams or in the band just wanted the experience to be "cool" or a part of something bigger than themselves. Honestly, there is nothing wrong with being on a team or investing lots of time in an extracurricular activity. I think there are lots of benefits to being in a sport. The question you have to ask yourself is if that sport or activity will benefit you ten or twenty years down the road. If the answer is no, then you really have to stop and think if it is indeed worth it to put your time and energy into that activity.

Chapter 3

Finding your strengths

"Everybody is a genius. If you judge a fish by its ability to climb a tree, it will live its whole life believing that it is stupid."

-Albert Einstein

In high school and college, the so-called "career centers" or "career counselors" were not very helpful to me. I'm sure they are helpful to some, and maybe I just had a bad experience, but I found that the best help for me came in reading lots of books, talking to lots of people, and trying lots of new things. One book I recommend is "Strength Finders" by Tom Rath. What is great about this book is that it focuses on helping you identify your strengths and shows you how to use this knowledge when pursuing a career.

There are so many people I know who ended up doing something that either they weren't really that good at or they didn't really enjoy all that much. The important thing about choosing a career path is to choose something that lines up with your strengths, passions, and abilities. Sometimes it's not necessarily fair to ask a child what they want to be when they grow up. They are still figuring out who they are as people, what they like/dislike and what intrigues them. At what age is someone

Finding Your Strengths

old enough to decide what they want to do when they grow up? This is not the easiest question to answer and probably not an exact science, but teenagers who choose a career path when they are fifteen or sixteen years old have a better chance of being prepared for that type of career than someone who waits until they are midway through college.

Part of growing up is figuring out your taste as a human and what makes you YOU. We discover our musical tastes, preferences in clothing, interest in sports, values in religion, romantic interests, types of friends we attract and what we enjoy in school. The list can go on and on...but all these things do not develop overnight, just like a decision to pick a career is often something that most college students are still trying to figure out.

Why is it that only 27 percent of college graduates actually end up in a career that utilizes their degree? My initial thought is that the other 73 percent did not do the hard work of figuring out both who they are and what they were passionate about before choosing their degree. It's possible that a good portion of these students were still figuring out some of this in college. There comes a time when making a decision to major in something that does not align with your career is both a waste of money and time.

So, does that mean that high school students must figure out their career path before college? In an ideal world, YES, however, most colleges are setup were you can take the first year or two of basics without even touching a concentrated class. Essentially, you can buy yourself some time if you still haven't decided on a career at this point in your life if you are going the college route.

To be fair, having a degree that doesn't align with your career isn't always a bad thing. Sometimes the idea of having a degree in general makes you more employable because it shows an employer that you completed something pretty difficult.

So how do you go about finding your likes and your strengths? The key is trying lots of things from an early age and being self-aware when you realize you are truly good at something.

Growing up, my parents signed me up for lots of sports. I tried soccer, baseball, gymnastics, hockey, and football. I remember being pretty horrible at all of these with the exception of hockey. But I knew I didn't enjoy it enough to pursue it professionally. For me, the idea of being a pro-athlete never crossed my mind. It was a simple choice to not care that much about sports because my strengths did not come from my athletic ability or my physicality. I was okay with this. It's important that if you have a weakness, you don't beat yourself up over it. Sometimes it's okay to accept that weakness and just move on to something you are good at.

One interest I had growing up was singing. I sang in the choir at school and at church. Occasionally, I would write songs, attend concerts, and geek out over anything musical. For a brief moment I was the lead singer of a band—that lasted about a month. While I thought the idea of doing something serious with singing would be fun, I had a hard time believing it could go anywhere since I couldn't play the guitar, and the few times I tried to learn I hated it. It was difficult to come to this decision but, ultimately, I decided that pursuing music would not be in the best interest of my career.

When I was in junior high and high school, I was very involved in two things: journalism at school and my youth group at church. It's funny because in both areas I was essentially coordinating and managing things. I slowly discovered that my strengths primarily lied in telling stories and leadership. As the newspaper editor, I was constantly scheduling stories and photo assignments between my peers. In my youth group, I was helping to book concerts, create videos and websites, and run sound for events. I was on the leadership council and enjoyed making things happen. I was slowly discovering that my strengths really were found in the logistical side of things and organization.

Finding your strengths is not something you can discover overnight. Once you have tried lots and lots of things, you will slowly discover the things you enjoy, the things you hate, the things that you are really good at and the things that are really difficult for you.

Maybe you have tried lots of things but you haven't evaluated your strengths. Go ahead and list all of your interests and evaluate which ones you are actually really good at. Sometimes it's difficult to think of all your interests without taking a personality test or career assessment test, which we will get into later in this book.

Perhaps you haven't really tried as many things as you would have hoped to at this stage in your life. Set a goal to try certain interests that you have been curious about but haven't tried yet.

Maybe you like the idea of being a chef but you don't know if you would be any good at it. Consider taking a cooking course in your community or enrolling in home economics at school. Even experimenting at home could help you discover if this is for you.

It could be likely that you fancy the idea of being a nurse but are clueless as to what that would actually be like. Consider volunteering at a local hospital where you can observe doctors and nurses at work. You will gain a firsthand experience and can even ask nurses what they think of their jobs.

Perhaps you want to be a lawyer but aren't sure if you would like it. Consider getting involved in your school's speech and debate classes where you can experience the pressure of a courtroom. If you end up loving speech and debate, then maybe you are on to something.

Exploring new things might mean taking a new elective class, signing up for a club or sport or even learning something online watching YouTube tutorials. There are so many things you can learn online with a few clicks of a button, it's not even funny.

When it comes to figuring out your interests and skills, the perfect time to do this is when you are a teenager. In school, there was a vast amount of electives, clubs, sports, and extracurricular activities anyone could be involved in. If you wanted to do ten things or one thing, it was really up to you. Don't wait until you are older to explore the many things that might interest you because the pressure of bills and adult-like responsibilities will soon follow.

Chapter 4

You're never too young

"When you are young, work to learn, not to earn."

-Rober Kiyosaki

When I was in seventh grade, I turned fourteen halfway through the year and found the only business in town that I knew of that would hire fourteen-year-olds…was a grocery store. I signed up almost the same week I was old enough and began the work of bagging groceries, cleaning floors and helping out wherever I was needed. This experience, while not my favorite, taught me the value of hard work and the value of a college education. I knew that if I didn't study hard and attend college, I too could end up like some of the people working in the store I despised. It wasn't a terrible job … it was just very repetitive in nature. This was something that terrified me. Now don't get me wrong, there is nothing horrible about working in a restaurant or retail store however, most of these jobs pay minimum wage and are very physically demanding. I knew that I wanted to make more than minimum wage and I wanted a job or career that would be challenging both creatively and mentally.

I was probably one of the only kids in my seventh grade class that had a job. I'm not necessarily recommending that teenagers get a job as young as I did, but

THE CAREER CHOSE ME

there is value in hard work at a young age, even if it means mowing lawns one summer. For me, the hard work and experience of working in a grocery store, restaurant, and retail store gave me every bit of knowledge that without a shadow of a doubt I did NOT want to do any of these jobs as an adult. I had more jobs as a teenager than almost any kid I knew, and this was essentially confirming my taste of what types of work I did and did not enjoy. I knew that I did not enjoy jobs with an emphasis on manual labor. I knew that I did not enjoy jobs that were repetitive in nature.

Here are some of the companies I worked for as a teenager:

>	Winn Dixie
>	Cici's Pizza
>	Chick-fil-a
>	CompUSA
>	Law Office
>	First Baptist Church of Hurst
>	AT&T
>	Pappadeaux Seafood Kitchen
>	Computer Repair Warehouse
>	Freelance Web Designer
>	Freelance DJ

If I had to do it over again, would I work all these jobs again? Maybe not. What I do know is that I put myself in a lot of situations and a lot of different work environments at a young age. All of these jobs gave me the energy and stamina to pursue higher learning and a career that was dependent on my interests. One of the reasons I worked so much during junior high and high school is because I wanted to be an adult *so* badly. I know it sounds funny but ever since I was little I wanted to be a grown-up. To me the idea of showing up at a job where you are needed sounded so cool to me. Not only that, I loved the idea of being able to take care of myself and buy my own clothes and drive to the movies when I wanted to. School always felt like a waste of time when I knew that once I graduated I wouldn't need half of what I was learning. Am I recommending that every teenager work a dozen jobs like I did…absolutely not. You should experience manual work early on so that you can know if you want to do that type of work for the rest of your life. If you don't want to work a job that is repetitive and requires manual labor, then this should hopefully light a fire within you and give you the drive to pursue college or a trade that matches what you do want to do.

Whenever I meet a teenager who has no idea what he/she wants to do for a living, I am almost assured that they haven't had that many experiences in the workforce.

Maybe you have had several jobs and have had similar experiences to what I have had. Let this be a reminder to you when you feel like giving up. There were many times in college when I didn't know if I could keep going. I remember one class in particular that I really struggled with and I honestly didn't know if I would pass. I was on the verge of failing the course when I decided to hunker down and study in the basement of the college library for an entire week. While I didn't ace this course, I did pass it and I relied on the motivation of my prior work experiences to keep going and not give up.

Perhaps you haven't had a job yet and you are curious about what it's like to enter the workforce. Consider creating a resume and applying for entry-level jobs in your area. Creating a resume when you haven't had any jobs can be difficult because employers often want to see prior work experience. Find ways to create a resume that shows your volunteer or leadership experience at school. You can list that you were the owner of a company if you mowed lawns for a summer. Don't discount even the smallest of jobs or work experience. If you aren't sure what your resume should look like, simply Google resume templates and you will get tons of examples that are easy to modify using Microsoft Word.

When it comes to finding entry-level jobs, Craigslist.org is a great website for finding work. Don't be afraid to inquire at local places you enjoy going to. Maybe you have a favorite clothing store or ice cream place you frequent. Ask the manager if there are any openings. A lot of times there may be openings at a company that aren't advertised. One reason these jobs aren't advertised is because the opening is so new that the manager or owner often hasn't had time to publicize it. When you do apply for a job, make sure to fill out the application as neatly as possible and call back two to three days later. If you are persistent and call back, you will get the attention of the owner/manager, and this is a quality that employers want to see.

Once you have landed a job and have worked there for several months, don't be afraid to quit and try a new job. Ideally, you would find a new job before you quit so that you will not have a gap in income if you are paying for your car insurance or phone bill. Typically, I would stay at a company for five to six months before quitting and working somewhere else. I could have stayed longer, but I found it more fun to work at different places, have new experiences, and make more money. Most of the time when I decided to work at a new company, it was generally a better job that paid more and gave me a unique experience.

Chapter 5

Pursue the impossible

"Genius is one percent inspiration, ninety-nine percent perspiration."

-*Thomas A. Edison*

You should pursue a job or career that, if you landed it today, you would be totally shocked and amazed that you are actually getting paid to do it. Life is too short to be an insurance salesman if in your heart of hearts you really want to work with animals. Imagine that you had to pick a career you would be stuck with for the next sixty years and you could not change your mind midway through. What would you pick to do? Oftentimes it can be easy to give up on a dream because it may require too much school or the odds are too big or your friends or family don't know if you have what it takes to make it in that field.

I remember when I was considering moving to Los Angeles to work in the film industry, I heard doubt from various people. They would raise questions such as, "What if you don't make it?" or "Do you have a backup plan just in case?" My answer was always, "I will make it and I don't have a backup plan because I will do whatever it takes to make it there." Not only did I make it in Los Angeles, but I'm thriving there, having worked on more than 50 movies in only five years. Were those questions valid? Perhaps. If I would have let those questions get to me, I might have never made the move.

There are certain jobs and career paths where you should proceed with caution before devoting your heart and soul into them. Maybe you want to be an actor, dancer, singer, or professional athlete and are unsure if it's worth pursuing such a high-risk career choice. The probability of making it as a professional athlete is very, very small, so you have to know this going into it and have feedback from your coaches, players, friends, family, and industry professionals on whether they think you have what it takes to be successful. Ask them to be brutally honest, and if most of them believe you have the gusto, then consider pursuing it. If, however, your coach isn't sure it's the smartest decision, you should really stop and listen to him/her and try to step back and evaluate yourself.

Being self-aware will help you tremendously when choosing to pursue something that is slightly risky.

If you think you can sing, record something and send it to five vocal coaches anonymously and ask for feedback. Ask them to be brutally honest and see if you have what it takes to be a singer. It's not enough to have your friends and family tell you that you're great and applaud every time you do karaoke.

I often write screenplays in my spare time because I have aspirations to someday make a film that I wrote. It's a very risky thing so I do it as a hobby, and there isn't that much pressure on me. When I complete a script, I send it to several script readers without my name on it so my identity doesn't influence them in any way. I want to get a professional's advice on whether or not they believe the script has merit. I ask for feedback and oftentimes they will provide positive/negative notes that I find are extremely helpful. If I were to rely on my own intuition of whether the script was good or bad I might be blinded to the potential problems in the story.

When it comes to dreaming big and pursuing your dreams, it's important to find success early on to build up the confidence you will need down the road. While I had never worked on a movie set until after college, I had produced hundreds of videos, written several screenplays, and was constantly learning everything I could in the film industry. I found success when many of these projects I had created were well-received by the audiences I was creating them for. This feedback gave me the confidence needed to move across the country and take a stab at an industry that was very difficult to break into. I had been writing, shooting, and editing videos for nearly a decade before I decided to take this to the next level. Sure, I could have moved to Los Angeles right after high school and avoided the financial costs of college, but I chose the college route and delayed my immediate entrance until I was ready.

A friend of mine is currently touring the states on a twenty-city tour with his band as I write this. I love his story because he was pursuing the impossible and then landed a record deal. It was too good to be true. Now his music is on the radio and he's playing in front of large crowds all over the world. Just two years ago he was sleeping in a shed in the backyard of his parents' house, living humbly, working on his music. He was willing to be poor and live frugally for the sake of pursuing his dreams.

A lot of people are afraid to pursue the impossible because they are afraid of the risks and possible hard times that come with such a pursuit.

It's definitely easier to get a dependable job that doesn't pay well that you hate than to pursue a career that is not 100 percent foolproof. It's possible that it could take years or decades to be successful in a career that seems far-fetched.

When I first moved to Los Angeles, I had no job lined up in the film industry. I was applying daily for dozens of jobs and had no response from anyone. I remember trying to even apply at local fast food places and getting nowhere because I didn't speak Spanish and I was overqualified. I finally decided to be a valet driver until I landed some film work. This was one of the toughest jobs I had ever had because I was constantly running to and from the parking garage like my life depended on it. I got to drive several celebrities' cars and even got to get concert tickets for Pierce Brosnan. This was a very humbling job because I had a college degree and had previously held a full-time job as a video producer. Now I was doing something that had nothing with my profession in an attempt to break into the film industry. It was super hard and sometimes I felt like giving up and going home. I look back on those tough times and am thankful I pushed through. I slowly landed film jobs that paid nothing more than $50 a day, then minimum wage, and then decent rates. This career transition didn't happen overnight and didn't come easily for me. There were many times I wasn't sure if I could pay my rent or find my next gig. Sometimes there would be weeks or months between projects where I was unemployed and bills would start to pile up. Thankfully, work always came and I was never late on any payments. The first two years of my career transition were extremely difficult, and I could see why a lot of people went to LA and left after a short while. I was essentially pursuing what I thought might be an impossible feat.

When you pursue the impossible, you have to be willing to take risks, live frugally and be resourceful. Sometimes you may have to temporarily take jobs that are not in your field simply to pay bills.

Chapter 6

Pick that ONE thing

"People think focus means saying yes to the thing you've got to focus on. But that's not what it means at all. It means saying no to the hundred other good ideas that there are."

-Steve Jobs

Growing up, you have the option of having lots of interests and extracurricular activities to be involved in. I know friends of mine who would be involved in several sports and still manage to participate in band and choir and the student council. As much as I admired them for juggling so many things, I never really understood the benefit of being stretched so thin. I made the decision in high school to focus as much as possible on journalism because I knew that I wanted to pursue a career that involved telling stories. I got involved in the newspaper in ninth grade and quickly became the editor the next year, and for the rest of my high school career I was busy taking pictures, writing articles, and managing a team of storytellers. What I enjoyed about this experience is that I got to focus on telling really good stories through words and photos, something that would translate to what I currently do now as a film producer.

THE CAREER CHOSE ME

Now, I'm not arguing to always pick one thing and that's it. There is, however, a benefit in life to not stretching yourself so thin and to really finding something that you can give 110 percentt to. Sure, I could have been on a sports team if I wanted to. Would it have taken time away from my journalism focus? Probably.

As a film producer, I hire lots of people for various positions, and occasionally the resumes I receive are very interesting. I once got a resume from a guy who was a photographer, DJ, singer, actor, and general handyman. Whenever I receive resumes that are very scattered, it tells me that the person isn't very focused and may not be skilled in any one area. This is not always the case, but most of the time it is. Who is to say that having lots of skills and abilities is a bad thing, it's not. You do have to be careful about highlighting that you do 20 things on your resume or on social media sites when your goal is to do one or two things.

After college, I got a job at a non-profit as a video producer. For this particular job I had to wear lots of hats. I wrote scripts, shot videos, edited videos, and managed multiple projects. As much as I liked doing lots of different things, I realized that I wasn't getting really good at one or two things because I was constantly doing ten things halfway. When I realized this, I made a change, and after five years of working for this non-profit, I left the world of video and moved to Los Angeles to work in the film industry where I would focus solely on producing and assistant directing. Where I used to be a team of one and do everything myself, now I work on films that have a crew size of thirty to 100 people per project and every person has a very specific job description. When I made this change to focus on one or two things, I began to get really good at those things and it really helped me to excel. It was tempting to pursue things I still knew how

Pick That One Thing

to do, such as editing, since I knew I could make money and could do this on the side. Because I didn't want to be an editor anymore, I quit editing cold turkey in an effort to focus on a few things.

Today, I still like to pursue other things outside of the two things I focus on as a producer or assistant director. I often write screenplays, build websites, blog, and come up with inventions. Even though I have these skills, I make a conscious effort to not list them all on my resume because I know it will make me look like I'm not focused.

People in hiring positions want to hire people who are laser focused to do one thing really, really well. If you can show people that you have experience doing that one thing for a long time, then the chances of you getting hired become much greater.

Experts are often deemed experts because they have spent years and sometimes decades devoting themselves to one area of discipline. Steve Irwin was known for being an expert in handling crocodiles. His expertise was so well-known that his name always coincided with "the crocodile hunter." It was almost like if you needed an expert on crocodiles, Steve was the guy to call. What if you were an expert like Steve and were so good at your job that people thought of you whenever they thought of that job?

I once hurt my back at work lifting lots of heavy equipment. I decided to see a chiropractor and was smart enough to ask around at my workplace. My inquiries led me to an expert. After he fixed my back, I was soon referring others to this miracle worker. If people had back problems, I would send them to this guy because he was synonymous with healing bodies.

I don't know about you, but if I hire a lawyer, plumber, carpenter, hair stylist, dentist, anyone at all, I want to hire the best I can possibly afford. I want to hire people I can trust. Essentially, I want to leave it to the experts.

It's not enough for you to say you want to be a lawyer someday. To succeed in this world, you have to be an expert in whatever career you choose. To make true changes in your field of discipline, you have to be laser focused and find that area of expertise you can excel in.

How does one become an expert in a field of study, you might ask?

First, you need to be a person who is always learning new things in that particular arena. Read as many books, articles, and blogs as you possibly can and don't ever give up on your thirst for knowledge. Find classes, workshops, or seminars that might pertain to your field of study and continue to investigate as much as you can.

Second, find an avenue to write about your findings as an expert. For some, this might mean starting a blog or posting insights on Facebook periodically. When you take that next step of writing down insights, you are allowing yourself to digest the information at a deeper level.

Third, search for a mentor in your field and consider apprenticing under them or even meeting on occasion to gather wisdom and guidance. Having a mentor will greatly increase your ability to head in the right direction when difficult decisions arise.

Fourth, find a way to practice your craft on a volunteer basis. If you are a lawyer, consider taking pro-bono cases. If you are a teacher, consider volunteering to sponsor a school organization. If you are an engineer, consider building a robot in your free time. You get the picture—don't let your paid work determine your level of success.

Finally, be really, really, really good at your job. Aim to be the best, and by posturing yourself to be the best, you will always be on the lookout to improve and be better.

Pick That One Thing

Being an expert in your field is more than being a know-it-all. By choosing to be an expert, you are choosing to allow success to find you in your career.

Chapter 7

Show me the money

"Never go into business purely to make money. If that's the motive, you're better off doing nothing."

-Richard Branson

How much money do you want to make when you get older? This is a question that sometimes arises when kids, teenagers, and adults try to figure out what they want to do in life. While it's important to make money, putting this question at the forefront can be a dangerous thing, especially when you are making a decision as big as choosing a career.

Deciding a career based solely on how much income you might possibly generate is essentially setting yourself up to live a life that is focused on "things" and what you can "get" from life. If you want to be really "happy," you should focus on what can you "do" to contribute to society.

Let's say you want to be a doctor because you want to make a lot of money. Being a doctor is great, but the reason for wanting to be a doctor should intrinsically be because you have a desire to help people. If you seriously have no desire to help people and are only in it for the money ... one of these days you will end up hating that job.

Let's take, for instance, the career path of a lawyer. Lawyers can make a lot of money, however, they have to spend a ton of time and money on law school, which comes after paying for a four-year college degree. I've met many people in my industry who used to be lawyers and hated it. I also know lots of lawyers and attorneys who love their work. The people who practiced law and changed careers realized that all the money wasn't worth a career that didn't excite them. Think about how much money and time was wasted when these "lawyers" changed careers.

I wouldn't mind making a lot of money someday, don't get me wrong. I'm in an industry that pays well if you land a certain job or start working on major projects. I started out volunteering on film projects, working for free, eventually working for $50 a day until I made it on my first feature film where I was paid minimum wage. It's so funny to think about because it was only five years ago that I had just started in this industry. Today, I make good wages and have a decent apartment. I'm not rich yet, but life is good and I couldn't be happier.

The secret to making money is to do what you love and be the best in that field. Yes, some industries make more money than other industries, but you have to be really, really sure you want to pursue that industry for the right reasons and not because of how rich it will make you.

Below is a list of the 100 Best Jobs, according to U.S. News & World Report [1].

#1 Dentist

    23,300 Projected Jobs | $152,700 Median Salary | .1% Unemployment Rate

#2 Nurse Practitioner

    44,700 Projected Jobs | $98,190 Median Salary | .7% Unemployment Rate

THE CAREER CHOSE ME

#3 Physician Assistant
28,000 Projected Jobs | $98,180 Median Salary | .6% Unemployment Rate

#4 Statistician
10,100 Projected Jobs | $80,110 Median Salary | .8% Unemployment Rate

#5 Orthodontist
1,500 Projected Jobs | $187,200 Median Salary | .1% Unemployment Rate

#6 Nurse Anesthetist
7,400 Projected Jobs | $157,140 Median Salary | .7% Unemployment Rate

#7 Pediatrician
3,600 Projected Jobs | $170,300 Median Salary | .6% Unemployment Rate

#8 Computer Systems Analyst
118,600 Projected Jobs | $85,800 Median Salary | 2.4% Unemployment Rate

#9 Obstetrician and Gynecologist
4,300 Projected Jobs | $187,200 Median Salary | .6% Unemployment Rate

#10 Oral and Maxillofacial Surgeon
1,200 Projected Jobs | $187,200 Median Salary | .6% Unemployment Rate

#11 Optometrist
11,000 Projected Jobs | $103,900 Median Salary | 1.6% Unemployment Rate

#12 Occupational Therapy Assistant
14,100 Projected Jobs | $157,870 Median Salary | .6% Unemployment Rate

#13 Software Developer
135,300 Projected Jobs | $98,260 Median Salary | 2% Unemployment Rate

#14 Surgeon
9,100 Projected Jobs | $187,200 Median Salary | .6% Unemployment Rate

#15 Nurse Midwife
1,300 Projected Jobs | $92,510 Median Salary | .7% Unemployment Rate

#16 Physical Therapist
71,800 Projected Jobs | $84,020 Median Salary | 1.1% Unemployment Rate

#17 Anesthesiologist
7,100 Projected Jobs | $187,200 Median Salary | 1.7% Unemployment Rate

#18 Physician
5,100 Projected Jobs | $187,200 Median Salary | .6% Unemployment Rate

#19 Psychiatrist
4,200 Projected Jobs | $187,200 Median Salary | 1.2% Unemployment Rate

#20 Mathematician
700 Projected Jobs | $111,110 Median Salary | .8% Unemployment Rate

Show Me The Money

#21 Prosthodontist
100 Projected Jobs | $119,740 Median Salary | .1% Unemployment Rate

#22 Software Developer
135,300 Projected Jobs | $98,260 Median Salary | 2% Unemployment Rate

#23 Occupational Therapist
30,400 Projected Jobs | $80,150 Median Salary | 1.3% Unemployment Rate

#24 Diagnostic Medical Sonographer
16,000 Projected Jobs | $68,970 Median Salary | .4% Unemployment Rate

#25 Podiatrist
1,400 Projected Jobs | $119,340 Median Salary | 1.7% Unemployment Rate

#26 Financial Advisor
73,900 Projected Jobs | $89,160 Median Salary | 2% Unemployment Rate

#27 Actuary
4,400 Projected Jobs | $97,070 Median Salary | .8% Unemployment Rate

#28 Speech-Language Pathologist
28,900 Projected Jobs | $73,410 Median Salary | 1.8% Unemployment Rate

#29 IT Manager
53,700 Projected Jobs | $131,600 Median Salary | 1.9% Unemployment Rate

#30 Psychologist
32,500 Projected Jobs | $94,590 Median Salary | 1.2% Unemployment Rate

#31 Web Developer
39,500 Projected Jobs | $64,970 Median Salary | 3.6% Unemployment Rate

#32 Dental Hygienist
37,400 Projected Jobs | $72,330 Median Salary | 1.2% Unemployment Rate

#33 Operations Research Analyst
27,600 Projected Jobs | $78,630 Median Salary | 2.6% Unemployment Rate

#34 Environmental Engineer
6,800 Projected Jobs | $84,560 Median Salary | .8% Unemployment Rate

#35 Computer Network Architect
12,700 Projected Jobs | $100,240 Median Salary | .6% Unemployment Rate

#36 Respiratory Therapist
14,900 Projected Jobs | $57,790 Median Salary | .6% Unemployment Rate

#37 Mechanical Engineer
14,600 Projected Jobs | $83,590 Median Salary | 1.6% Unemployment Rate

#38 Physical Therapist Assistant
31,900 Projected Jobs | $55,170 Median Salary | 4% Unemployment Rate

THE CAREER CHOSE ME

#39 Accountant

142,400 Projected Jobs | $67,190 Median Salary | 2.5% Unemployment Rate

#40 Medical and Health Services Manager

56,300 Projected Jobs | $94,500 Median Salary | 1.2% Unemployment Rate

#41 Database Administrator

13,400 Projected Jobs | $81,710 Median Salary | 1% Unemployment Rate

#42 Massage Therapist

36,500 Projected Jobs | $38,040 Median Salary | 2% Unemployment Rate

#43 Occupational Therapy Aide

2,700 Projected Jobs | $27,800 Median Salary | .6% Unemployment Rate

#44 Chiropractor

7,900 Projected Jobs | $64,440 Median Salary | .8% Unemployment Rate

#45 Cartographer

3,600 Projected Jobs | $61,880 Median Salary | 3.6% Unemployment Rate

#46 Orthotist and Prosthetist

1,900 Projected Jobs | $64,430 Median Salary | 1.7% Unemployment Rate

#47 School Psychologist

30,500 Projected Jobs | $70,580 Median Salary | 1.2% Unemployment Rate

#48 Financial Manager

37,700 Projected Jobs | $117,990 Median Salary | 2% Unemployment Rate

#49 Pharmacist

9,100 Projected Jobs | $121,500 Median Salary | 1.7% Unemployment Rate

#50 Cardiovascular Technologist

11,500 Projected Jobs | $54,880 Median Salary | 1.4% Unemployment Rate

#51 Marriage and Family Therapist

5,000 Projected Jobs | $48,6000 Median Salary | .6% Unemployment Rate

#52 Information Security Analyst

14,800 Projected Jobs | $90,120 Median Salary | 3.9% Unemployment Rate

#53 Business Operations Manager

151,100 Projected Jobs | $97,730 Median Salary | 3.9% Unemployment Rate

#54 Optician

17,800 Projected Jobs | $34,840 Median Salary | 1.6% Unemployment Rate

#55 Industrial Psychologist

400 Projected Jobs | $77,350 Median Salary | 1.2% Unemployment Rate

#56 Radiation Therapist

2,300 Projected Jobs | $80,220 Median Salary | 1.7% Unemployment Rate

Show Me The Money

#57 Hearing Aid Specialist

1,600 Projected Jobs | $49,600 Median Salary | 1.4% Unemployment Rate

#58 Civil Engineer

23,600 Projected Jobs | $82,220 Median Salary | 1.5% Unemployment Rate

#59 Clinical Laboratory Technician

29,000 Projected Jobs | $38,970 Median Salary | 1.9% Unemployment Rate

#60 Computer Support Specialist

88,800 Projected Jobs | $62,250 Median Salary | 3.7% Unemployment Rate

#61 Lawyer

43,800 Projected Jobs | $115,820 Median Salary | 1.1% Unemployment Rate

#62 Clinical Social Worker

30,900 Projected Jobs | $52,380 Median Salary | 2.1% Unemployment Rate

#63 Home Health Aide

348,400 Projected Jobs | $21,920 Median Salary | 6.4% Unemployment Rate

#64 Interpreter and Translator

17,500 Projected Jobs | $44,190 Median Salary | 4% Unemployment Rate

#65 Wind Turbine Technician

4,800 Projected Jobs | $51,050 Median Salary | 5.1% Unemployment Rate

#66 Marketing Manager

18,200 Projected Jobs | $128,750 Median Salary | 2.8% Unemployment Rate

#66 Marketing Manager

18,20 Projected Jobs | $128,750 Median Salary | 2.8% Unemployment Rate

#67 Audiologist

3,800 Projected Jobs | $74,890 Median Salary | 2.8% Unemployment Rate

#68 Medical Records Technician

29,000 Projected Jobs | $37,110 Median Salary | 2.4% Unemployment Rate

#69 Management Analyst

103,400 Projected Jobs | $81,320 Median Salary | 3.2% Unemployment Rate

#70 Veterinarian

6,900 Projected Jobs | $88,490 Median Salary | .4% Unemployment Rate

#71 Financial Analyst

32,300 Projected Jobs | $80,310 Median Salary | 2.1% Unemployment Rate

#72 High School Teacher

55,900 Projected Jobs | $57,200 Median Salary | 2% Unemployment Rate

#73 Genetic Counselor

700 Projected Jobs | $72,090 Median Salary | 3.1% Unemployment Rate

THE CAREER CHOSE ME

#74 Substance Abuse and Behavioral Disorder Counselor

21,200 Projected Jobs | $39,980 Median Salary | 2.8% Unemployment Rate

#75 Physical Therapist Aide

19,500 Projected Jobs | $25,120 Median Salary | 4% Unemployment Rate

#76 Market Research Analyst

92,300 Projected Jobs | $62,150 Median Salary | 3.1% Unemployment Rate

#77 Medical Secretary

108,200 Projected Jobs | $33,040 Median Salary | 3.8% Unemployment Rate

#78 MRI Technologist

3,500 Projected Jobs | $67,720 Median Salary | 1.4% Unemployment Rate

#79 Insurance Sales Agent

43,500 Projected Jobs | $48,200 Median Salary | 2.3% Unemployment Rate

#80 Cost Estimator

18,700 Projected Jobs | $60,390 Median Salary | 1.7% Unemployment Rate

#81 Medical Assistant

138,900 Projected Jobs | $30,590 Median Salary | 3.3% Unemployment Rate

#82 Dietitian and Nutritionist

11,000 Projected Jobs | $57,910 Median Salary | 3.5% Unemployment Rate

#83 Petroleum Engineer

3,400 Projected Jobs | $129,990 Median Salary | 4% Unemployment Rate

#84 Loan Officer

24,500 Projected Jobs | $63,430 Median Salary | 3.2% Unemployment Rate

#85 Personal Care Aide

458,100 Projected Jobs | $20,980 Median Salary | 7.5% Unemployment Rate

#86 Veterinary Technologist and Technician

17,900 Projected Jobs | $31,800 Median Salary | 1.8% Unemployment Rate

#87 Maintenance and Repair Worker

83,500 Projected Jobs | $36,630 Median Salary | 4.2% Unemployment Rate

#88 Nuclear Medicine Technologist

300 Projected Jobs | $73,360 Median Salary | 1.4% Unemployment Rate

#89 Construction Manager

17,800 Projected Jobs | $87,400 Median Salary | 2.5% Unemployment Rate

#90 Patrol Officer

34,200 Projected Jobs | $58,320 Median Salary | 1% Unemployment Rate

#91 Computer Systems Administrator

30,200 Projected Jobs | $77,810 Median Salary | 3.1% Unemployment Rate

Show Me The Money

#92 Radiologic Technologist
17,200 Projected Jobs | $56,670 Median Salary | 1.4% Unemployment Rate

#93 Surgical Technologist
14,700 Projected Jobs | $44,330 Median Salary | 1.4% Unemployment Rate

#94 Epidemiologist/Medical Scientist
400 Projected Jobs | $69,450 Median Salary | 1.9% Unemployment Rate

#95 Biochemist
2,800 Projected Jobs | $82,150 Median Salary | 2.1% Unemployment Rate

#96 Child and Family Social Worker
19,000 Projected Jobs | $42,350 Median Salary | 2.1% Unemployment Rate

#97 Mental Health Counselor
26,400 Projected Jobs | $41,880 Median Salary | 2.8% Unemployment Rate

#98 Paramedic
58,500 Projected Jobs | $31,980 Median Salary | 1.3% Unemployment Rate

#99 Sales Manager
19,000 Projected Jobs | $113,860 Median Salary | 2.8% Unemployment Rate

#100 Dental Assistant
58,600 Projected Jobs | $35,980 Median Salary | 2.8% Unemployment Rate

One thing you can immediately notice about this list is the vast amount of technical and medical professions that are in high demand. Again, this is not to say pursuing one of these 100 careers is a sure bet, but you are increasing your chances of a high-paying job if you do. Don't get discouraged if you don't see a career you are considering on this list; that doesn't necessarily mean anything. My career is nowhere near being on this list because the unemployment rate is so high among film professionals.

Perhaps you value the idea of having a job that is in high demand, has a good median salary, and shows an overall low unemployment rate. If these are values of yours, then choosing a job on this list can't hurt. Maybe you value the idea of a high income more than you value pursuing something you are really passionate about. That's okay, many people have jobs that are reliable, pay well, and provide for them and their families all the comforts they need. At the end of the day, a good percentage of these people don't depend on their job to express their passions or artistic freedom.

I know many people who hold full-time office jobs and write screenplays at night or on weekends in an attempt to someday sell a script. This full-time office job for them is only a means to an end, but it's not the end in and of itself. I've met people who work odd jobs during the day, such as driving for Uber or working at a coffeehouse, and this freedom allows them to pursue artistic careers such as acting or singing. This goes to show you that even if you end up taking Job A, you can still pursue Job B until Job B can provide for you financially.

Perhaps what is really important to you is having a family, kids, going on vacations, and attending sporting events. The idea of having a career that aligns with your skills just doesn't resonate with you all that much at this point in your life. Maybe you aren't really that picky and you just want a job that can afford you a certain lifestyle. A list like the one above can come in real handy when you are having trouble crossing off careers and figuring out what you want to do.

Even if you aren't super passionate about any one particular job, you more than likely have some interests and you should pursue a job that falls in line with those interests. Remember, you could be stuck with this job for the next fifty years of your life. In school, you often take multiple subjects and most of the time you gravitate towards one or two of these classes as your favorites. Do you have any favorites now? Perhaps you like math and science but hate history and English. Do these interests tell you anything?

Perhaps you like the idea of working in the medical field. Again, as you can see from the list above, there are

Show Me The Money

tons of jobs in the medical field that pay well and have a very low unemployment rate. Even if you don't know the specific medical job you want, choosing to pursue medicine if that is an interest of yours could turn out to be a good investment compared to other college majors.

Another thing to consider when thinking about salaries and jobs is what kind of lifestyle you want to have. Do you want to barely get by and live paycheck to paycheck, or do you want to have a job that allows you to travel, go on vacations, and buy nice things whenever you choose?

When choosing a career and thinking about salaries, you can compare the risk of this decision to the risk of making an investment in a stock or a company. Let's say I were to invest $10,000 in a company or stock. Before I make the decision to invest, I am going to do the research needed to make an informed decision because I don't want to lose my money. I will look at the history of the stock and see where it had growths or losses over the years. I might try to read articles about this particular stock or company, talk to a stock broker ,or look at data online. It would be foolish for me to invest on a whim without doing the necessary research. When it comes to choosing a career and looking at salaries, don't be afraid to do the hard research needed before making the decision to go one way or the other.

Footnote:

[1] "100 Best Jobs of 2017," US News, https://money.usnews.com/careers/best-jobs/rankings/the-100-best-jobs, (2017)

Chapter 8

Going undercover

"Shoot for the moon. Even if you miss, you'll land among the stars."

-Les Brown

When it comes to finding the right career, make a conscious effort to investigate as much as you can about as many careers as you are interested in. Even if you are only slightly interested in a specific career, don't rule it out without spending the time needed to learn about it. You never know when the career you were only mildly interested in quickly becomes the career that you start to lean towards once you do your investigation. Know that it's possible you might have more than one career or job in your lifetime, even if you decide to not choose a specific career, the knowledge of all the careers you explored could come in handy if you decide to change careers at some point.

Growing up, I loved watching spy movies. There was something about the strategy involved in their recon that I found fascinating. Imagine for a moment that you are a spy going undercover to take down a rogue world leader. What kind of investigation would you put together? You wouldn't take this assignment lightly. It would be a team effort that would depend on multiple sources and months, if not years, of research and data.

For fun, imagine that you are the spy or detective to the future job you want to have. What would that look like? How could you mine for data? Who would you speak to? Where could you get information about this or that job that is out there? Make the investigation fun and know that it could take months or years until you stumble upon that magical job description that was made for you.

Upon your investigation, ask your dad, mom, aunts, uncles, friends, teachers, bosses if they enjoy their jobs. If they do, ask them what part of it they enjoy and what part of it not so much. If they don't enjoy their jobs, ask them why they are currently in that career. Did they get stuck doing it? Maybe you will discover a job that you never knew existed by asking someone what he/she does and then shadow them at work one day.

All it took for me was meeting a film producer when I was seven to decide I wanted to be in that industry. Most people already know what a teacher does so it's a pretty easy thing to understand, but there are so many jobs out there that young people have no idea what they entail without getting a little bit of hands-on experience.

I periodically get email inquiries from recent grads who wish to intern with me. I'm not able to answer all these emails, but sometimes I have an opening and I make an effort to reply to the candidates. This past summer I was producing a movie and brought an intern onto the film. The pay I promised was nothing for the first week, and if things went well, he would be paid a salary for the duration of the project, which ended up being six weeks of work. Things ended up going well for this intern and we were able to hire him after his first week of proving to us that he was a valuable asset to the project. This guy had never been on a film set before and was only a year into college. The experience he got on this film set was invaluable because he got to see everything firsthand. I'll be honest and say I wish I had that experience when I was in college. Some days I kick myself for not working on a real film set earlier like my intern did. To think about what I could have learned about the different positions and jobs could have really fast-tracked my career. What amazes me about this intern is that he didn't apply to a post I had made on the internet. He did the hard research of looking up companies and sending cold emails, hoping someone would reply. I'm sure he contacted several companies that never responded, but this didn't stop him from moving forward. Sometimes finding the right opportunity takes research, persistence, and a bit of creativity.

When you are being inquisitive, don't be afraid to consider a job that no one has ever heard of. The other day I was on LinkedIn looking for jobs and I stumbled across a job titled "Project Analyst." The title sounded interesting. I quickly did some digging and realized it was for someone who was really into accounting ... which isn't me. I had never heard of this specific job before and even today I'm open to exploring other jobs in my current field if I happen to be a good fit.

Being open to jobs and careers will make it a lot easier to stumble into just the right one.

Reading books on the career(s) you are interested in is another way to investigate the job. This will give you a sense if it is indeed something you want to pursue.

When I was in high school, I was living in Texas and there weren't that many film shoots around for me to visit. I found the next best thing by watching the behind the scenes vignettes on the DVDs of my favorite movies. As soon as I finished a movie I would make sure to watch all the bonus features. This was my chance to learn as much as I could and get a glimpse into the life of filmmaking. Sometimes you have to be creative when it comes to learning about your career. There are many jobs that require special security clearances that would make it impossible for you to shadow. Your best bet in that situation is to read articles, books, and blogs about those specific jobs.

I was lucky enough when I was in elementary school to join a special program that allowed kids a firsthand look at what it was like to work for the city. I got to ride in a fire truck, ambulance, police car, and observe an operating 911 station.

I remember being super excited about this experience because I knew that it was a privilege to ride in these types of vehicles.

One way to investigate careers is to visit your parents' or relatives' places of work. I can remember doing that on many occasions and getting a firsthand experience of what it was like.

Once when I was little, I accompanied my dad to help run sound for several events he was volunteering for at my church. I fell in love with the process and years later began to run sound myself for a youth group I was involved in. The interest in running sound came from being with my dad, who was an expert in the audio field. I continued to run sound for many years, even later working as a DJ in college. I found that being able to run sound for organizations and companies was a valuable skill set to have because not many people had this knowledge. For me, running sound became a valuable way for me to contribute and volunteer in a way that got me excited. While I was running sound I realized that even though I enjoyed it as a hobby, it was not something I wanted to do professionally. Sometimes hobbies

THE CAREER CHOSE ME

turn into careers and sometimes they just remain hobbies. Regardless of whether or not I was to pursue this as a career, I was able to investigate the field of sound and acoustics and learn firsthand what I liked and disliked about it.

Chapter 9

Invest in YOU

"You have brains in your head. You have feet in your shoes. You can steer yourself any direction you choose. You're on your own. And you know what you know. And YOU are the one who'll decide where to go."

-Dr. Seuss

Choosing a career path is perhaps one of the biggest decisions you will ever make in life, next to who you will marry or what religion you will choose to follow. And to think that so many people take this decision very lightly compared to these other decisions. Many people date for years before ever getting married. They want to make sure they're with the right person and they spend a ton of time figuring out who this person is and what their likes/dislikes are. Many people I know read or studied a certain religion before choosing what to follow and believe. Some people have even spent years growing up in a church/synagogue/mosque before deciding to follow a certain religion later in life, even though they may have been involved in a religion from a very young age.

We take relationships and religion very seriously when it comes to making these choices, and yet sometimes the idea of choosing a career is like picking a name out of a hat. Teachers are cool, I think I'll be a teacher–and that's that.

What if you spent serious time learning about certain careers, narrowing down options, and talking to experts? What if choosing a career wasn't a decision based on a whim or an idea, but based on experience and research? People decide they want to get married based on their past experiences and shared values, so why can't this be the same with choosing a career?

What if you dedicated one hour every Sunday to your future work life? This hour could be spent doing research online, watching videos about certain jobs, listening to podcasts on topics that align with the job you are seeking, talking to experts in the field, shadowing someone at their place of work, etc.

We've all heard stories of people who have gone off and eloped after only dating for a few weeks. While this is not necessarily a wise idea, it can work, but could also set a couple up for failure. If your career choice held as much weight as who you will marry, you will be putting yourself in a position to have a better outcome.

Chances are you will spend more time in your place of work than you will with your future family. The average person spends close to 92,120 hours in their lifetime doing "work." Think long and hard about that number because you want to make sure that the thing you do during those thousands of hours is something you enjoy, something you care about, something that excites you, and something you were born to do.

If you are getting cold feet about a certain career choice, that's probably a good thing. That means you are taking this decision seriously and don't know 100 percent if it's the correct one. When do you know if you've picked the right career? Maybe you can't know this until you are in the middle of it. I was thirty-years-old before I absolutely knew I had picked the right career path. In college, I thought I was picking the right career, and post-college I kind of thought I was doing what I wanted to do. It wasn't until later that I landed several jobs where I was able to both excel and enjoy the experience. I feel grateful because I know many people who never figure out what they were made to do. They go from job to job to job and are constantly in a state of flux.

Think about any thing or person you love. If you love this thing or person, you are apt to want to spend time with them and get to know them. Now, I know it sounds silly to be in love with your career, but you want to love what you do, don't you? Maybe loving what you do for a living will mean you will, at some point, have to choose not to love other things, or love them less. When I was little, I spent time collecting baseball cards, building Legos, and playing video games. These were the things I loved as a seven-year-old. I could have hung on to these loves through my adulthood and tried to keep loving them, but those loves would have served as a distraction to what is really important to me today. It's funny because I know adults who still play with action figures, play video games, and dress up as medieval characters on the weekends. There is nothing wrong with having these hobbies but, for me, having too many interests would make it difficult to have balance in my life.

Let's go back to the idea of spending 92,100 hours of your life doing this idea we call "work." What if you spent just a small fraction of your teenage and college years learning about and investigating your career? Even just one percent of this gigantic number averages ninety-two hours, which spread out over months and years could be about two hours a week for a year or one hour a week for two years. Worthy investment? You might be getting to the point where you feel you have no time to investigate a career. Maybe you are swamped with school assignments, work, and a million things you are involved in. I would argue that you have to start scheduling blocks of time to investigate. That might mean dropping a sport or club in order to get serious and focus. If you use Google calendar, create a recurring event for one hour a week dedicated to learning about your future career. Simply having the goal and writing it down will increase your chances of following through instead of watching another show on Netflix.

If you think back to all the many things and activities you loved growing up, chances are you spent a considerable amount of time on each of these things. I can't begin to count the number of hours I spent playing with Legos as a kid–it must have been a lot because I built an entire Lego city that I kept under my bed on a huge piece of plywood. Spending lots of time on the things you loved came naturally. No one had to convince you to spend time playing video games–it came out of a natural want of enjoyment when playing that game. So when we talk about work and falling in love with it, it's possible that you might not initially want to spend all this time investigating a career you may or may not end up in. For some, this might sound fun, and for others, not so much. As you get older, some things will naturally grow on you and your likes will develop. I remember hating avocados when I was little because they looked gross. Today, I love everything avocado– especially guacamole. Even if you aren't crazy about the idea of spending time investigating a career, go ahead and do it anyway. Try it for a month or two and see if you get anything out of it.

Chapter 10

The college dilemma

"Education is the most powerful weapon we can use to change the world."

-Nelson Mandela

High school teachers spend years preparing students to be college-ready. Some students even find themselves in college-prep academies instead of a typical high school. Most of these schools pressure students to meet certain test scores so that they can qualify to attend certain colleges, giving the high schools the funding they need to keep on going. It's a funny cycle, and sometimes a sad one, that values test scores and memorizing lots of data over actual learning. While you or I may not agree with the way schools operate, the chance of us changing the system is very slim but not impossible. Nevertheless, flawed schools exist and we must accept this flawed entity and find ways to work within the system. To be fair, schools aren't the only imperfect entity. Life is full of organizations, companies, and systems that are imperfect. It would be odd if I refused to get a driver's license simply because the line at the DMV was so long and the clerk was rude to me. If you can accept a flawed system and realize its imperfections, you will allow yourself to not depend on any one system when it comes to learning and education.

When I chose to attend college during my junior year of high school, I knew in the back of my head I wanted to do as many things outside of school as possible and learn about my craft in new and interesting ways. For me, it wasn't enough to depend on a flawed system to teach me everything I needed to know. I made sure that once I enrolled in college, I would make as many film projects outside of class as possible, volunteer with various organizations, and devour as many books as I could that were not required for school. I believe this mentality is integral to where I am at today.

While college is an easy answer for many, it's still a dilemma and a big decision for a vast amount of high school juniors and seniors. Students are often put in a position to decide if they are going to college, which one will it be, and what major will they choose. It can be a lot of pressure for any seventeen- or eighteen-year-old to deal with. Students who decide not to pursue college or don't have a major picked out are often met with opposition by their friends, teachers, and parents, who question their reasoning to not make a decision or not to pursue a college. The pressure for some is too much, and for many it can be a bit overwhelming.

Today, more and more young people are choosing to NOT attend college or leave college early after a year or two into it. Twenty years ago, college was a must, but today you can get a pretty decent career without formal education as long as you learn on your own, use the internet, and are resourceful.

Let's say you want to be a web designer. Yes, you can learn code and design in college, but you can also learn it online and take coding courses using sites like Lynda.com. Essentially, you can be a self-taught web designer if you really wanted to. Imagine Joe Smith at Company X needs a website for his company. Joe doesn't care whether or not the potential web designer has a college degree. The only thing Joe cares about is the designer's portfolio (how many websites he has designed) and communication skills.

How do you determine if your career merits a college degree? The best thing to do is to ask people currently working in that field if they think college is imperative to landing a job in that specific industry and what level of schooling they recommend if so. I can guarantee you that you will get a mix of answers from people who find themselves in artistic careers such as film, music, design, etc. I sometimes regret attending film school because I was able to learn a lot of what I currently know by just working on film sets.

Let's say you want to start your own business. Maybe you have an idea for a new product or you want to open up a new coffee shop where you live. Getting an MBA or business degree could benefit you in your pursuit, however, there are a lot of entrepreneurs who are self-taught and have no formal college education whatsoever. You really have to weigh the pros and cons and decide if college is right for you and if it is worth the years and money you will spend.

Granted, there is value in attending college simply for the experience, additional learning, and connections you will make. I met some of my best friends in college and had some of the most transformational experiences there. For me, college was a time of personal growth, discovery, and connections. Even though I was learning about film and what that entails, I was also learning about other subjects on a broader level. Perhaps the biggest thing I learned at college was really discovering who I was and learning how to be disciplined and pursue a goal.

Another benefit to attending college is the potential increase in salary you could have.

"College graduates, on average, earned 56% more than high school grads in 2015, according to data compiled by the Economic Policy Institute." -USA TODAY[1]

So even if you aren't 100 percent sure you need college, you are increasing your chances of success for whatever career you end up in simply by attending.

Online colleges have been ever increasing, so even if you hate the idea of moving out of your parents' house and attending a traditional school, you have the opportunity to learn by taking online courses from the comfort of home or even when traveling abroad. This could be a great alternative for someone who still hasn't picked out a major but doesn't want to miss out on taking basic college courses. You can always attend an online college or local junior college for the first year or two and then transfer these credits to a public or private university.

Another thing to consider when choosing colleges is to think about taking a leap year. The leap year concept is a growing one and many students are finding value in taking internships or traveling overseas before they take the leap to invest another four or five years into intense schooling. Former President Barack Obama's oldest daughter, Malia, decided to take a leap year before attending college. Funny enough she interned down the street from me at a Hollywood agency because she wants to work in film.

Footnote:

[1] Christopher S. Rugaber, The Associated Press "Pay gap between college grads and everyone else at a record," https://www.usatoday.com/story/money/2017/01/12/pay-gap-between-college-grads-and-everyone-else-record/96493348/ (Jan. 12, 2017).

Chapter 11

Do what excites you

"People always ask you, 'What's your dream job?' This is my dream job. It really is a dream opportunity to have your own nationwide daily sports talk show for an hour."

-Adam Schein

When I was little, I participated in a school competition where we got to come up with inventions. To me, this was the most exciting activity in the world at the time because it challenged me in a whole new way that math and history class couldn't even come close to. I was forced to come up with something out of nothing. I was challenged to create a new way of doing something. My invention wasn't life changing, and it certainly didn't take off, but for your typical second grader, it was the thrill of doing something groundbreaking that was exciting to me. This is my first memory of really getting excited about doing work. This desire to invent things has stayed with me to this day. I have over a dozen inventions and apps that I have conceptualized and I'm always trying to get one of them off the ground.

    I have found over the years that I get excited about solving problems, managing logistics, and being involved in groundbreaking projects. I get excited about starting a new project and bringing it to life. Film is the perfect career for me because it is always changing and the challenges are constantly new. Every new film I work on is essentially a new startup company that has a new set of founders, employees, and its own unique story.

Think back to when you were little and what got you energized. Does that event or thing have any way of helping inform your decision to pursue a certain type of career? If you like consistency and if you like learning, then being a teacher may be a good fit for you. If you like the idea of helping people and listening to problems, then being a counselor might be your thing.

The formula is simple:

Step 1:

Figure out what excites you.

Step 2:

Take this excitement and see what careers fall into this area.

Step 3:

Do that career.

Now, I may be oversimplifying things, but I can guarantee that people who love what they do can trace this love back to a moment in their youth that got them excited about that type of work. It's interesting how our earliest childhood memories can be so influential later in life. One minute you might be playing with Nerf guns in the backyard, and the next minute you are enrolling in

Do What Excites You

the Army. That's what's so great about growing up — you learn about life through play.

As a kid, there is no such thing as work other than the chores your parents force on you and the homework you have from school. Every free moment as a kid is dedicated to "play." Play is this idea that you can dream, create, make-believe, compete, or build something incredible. Every part of play can be traced to a feeling that you resonate with. I used to love playing with Legos and building cities because it let me create something from nothing. I also used to love selling lemonade to my neighbors because it made me feel like I owned a company. Even though playing with Legos and setting up a lemonade stand might seem small, and were small to some degree, the feelings I had when I did both of those things are the same feelings I have today, only on a grander scale. Today, I love creating things from nothing and I enjoy the idea of owning my own company. The only difference is that instead of Legos and lemonade, I develop scripts with directors and attempt to own companies. While I may not be 100 percent successful at either creating something from nothing or owning companies, I don't let this discourage me from pursuing my dreams and chasing the same types of play I enjoyed when I was five.

If I were to talk to a five-year-old today about their future adult career, I would tell them not to worry about it and to focus on play. I would encourage them to play with as many different things as possible, try sports, explore music, dance, and photography. The more you explore and play, the more you will realize your tastes and likes/dislikes. Now, most of you reading this are much older than five, and yet some of you may have failed at playing and exploring as much as you could when you were little. It's never too late to play, explore, and try new things.

THE CAREER CHOSE ME

There is a story I discovered on the internet that really fits into this chapter.

[1] *The first day of school, our professor introduced himself and challenged us to get to know someone we didn't already know. I stood up to look around when a gentle hand touched my shoulder.*

I turned around to find a wrinkled, little old lady beaming up at me with a smile that lit up her entire being.

She said, "Hi, handsome. My name is Rose. I'm eighty-seven years old. Can I give you a hug?"

I laughed and enthusiastically responded, "Of course you may!" And she gave me a giant squeeze.

"Why are you in college at such a young, innocent age?" I asked.

She jokingly replied, "I'm here to meet a rich husband, get married, and have a couple of kids.»

"No, seriously," I asked. I was curious what may have motivated her to be taking on this challenge at her age.

"I always dreamed of having a college education and now I'm getting one!" she told me.

After class, we walked to the student union building and shared a chocolate milkshake.

We became instant friends. Every day for the next three months we would leave class together and talk nonstop. I was always mesmerized listening to this "time machine" as she shared her wisdom and experience with me.

Over the course of the year, Rose became a campus icon and she easily made friends wherever she went. She loved to dress up and she reveled in the attention bestowed upon her from the other students. She was living it up.

Do What Excites You

At the end of the semester, we invited Rose to speak at our football banquet.

I'll never forget what she taught us. She was introduced and stepped up to the podium. As she began to deliver her prepared speech, she dropped her three by five cards on the floor.

Frustrated and a little embarrassed, she leaned into the microphone and simply said, "I'm sorry I'm so jittery. I gave up beer for Lent and this whiskey is killing me!"

As we laughed, she cleared her throat and began. "We do not stop playing because we are old; we grow old because we stop playing. If you are nineteen years old and lie in bed for one full year and don't do one productive thing, you will turn twenty years old. If I am eighty-seven years old and stay in bed for a year and never do anything, I will turn eighty-eight. Anybody can grow older. That doesn't take any talent or ability. The idea is to grow up by always finding opportunity in change. Have no regrets. The elderly usually don't have regrets for what we did, but rather for things we did not do. The only people who fear death are those with regrets."

She concluded her speech by courageously singing "The Rose."

She challenged each of us to study the lyrics and live them out in our daily lives.

At the year's end, Rose finished the college degree she had begun all those years ago.

One week after graduation, Rose died peacefully in her sleep.

Footnote:

[1] Monsieur, "87 Year Old Woman Named Rose," http://www.kindspring.org/story/view.php?sid=6528, (April 10, 2010).

Chapter 12

Beware the robots

"The job market of the future will consist of those jobs that robots cannot perform. Our blue-collar work is pattern recognition, making sense of what you see. Gardeners will still have jobs because every garden is different. The same goes for construction workers. The losers are white-collar workers, low-level accountants, brokers, and agents."

-Michio Kaku

Robots are coming and they are slowly going to take over certain jobs that for the longest time were manned by humans. They won't necessarily take over the most exciting jobs, but they will slowly make it more and more difficult to obtain an entry-level job. You might have been to a restaurant where you ordered on a screen without talking to a cashier—that's one less cashier this company had to hire. Your future job or career could be replaced by a machine so it's important that you think long and hard before jumping into a career that could be eliminated in the near future.

I studied journalism in high school, which was when the internet was growing. I realized that print journalism was slowly dying and that to pursue this type of career post high school could be a dangerous thing. I was aware that the field of journalism was changing and I didn't want to be in a career that was on the verge of extinction. Think about bookstores; will they be around in ten years? Maybe. Maybe not. If you want to own a bookstore, you need to be careful because the trend of reading books on Kindles and iPads is ever increasing.

Don't let this idea of robots scare you too much, but it is important to remember that a good portion of jobs in the future will no longer exist simply because they will become automated.

Here is a list[1] of jobs that are being taken over by robots and computers:

-Assembly-line and factory workers
-Bus drivers, taxi drivers, and truck drivers
-Phone operators, telemarketers, and receptionists
-Cashiers
-Bank tellers and clerks
-Packing, stockroom, and warehouse moving
-Pharmacists
-Analysts and researchers
-Journalists and reporters
-Pilots
-Bartenders
-Stock traders
-Postal workers
-Doctors, anesthesiologists, and surgeons
-Soldiers and guards
-Travel agents
-Chefs and cooks
-Bomb squad
-Hotel staff and room service

This does not mean every and all jobs in this category. For example, the military uses drones that are unmanned, but commuter airlines will still rely on humans for a long time to come. If picking a job that could be taken over by the robot population scares you, then be thankful. It's much better to be scared away from a job because of the likelihood of it someday not existing rather than pursuing it full force, not ever knowing this possibility could even exist.

I love watching videos on Facebook and YouTube that show robots at work. It's fascinating to think that a machine can walk and talk like a human and even learn things. Amazon is one of the few companies that has figured out a robotic system that makes packaging an order almost seamless, depending mainly on robots and human drivers to get their orders processed. As I write this book, driverless cars are on the rise and the industry is changing rapidly. It's possible that someday you could have a robot delivering packages to your door. While it's fascinating to think about the amazing things robots can and will do in the future, and what industries they will reach, it's a very frightening thing to think of them taking over civilian jobs.

Anyone can lose their job at any time. Job security is great, but you should never depend on a company to be the security blanket for you or your family. Thousands of people get laid off each year for any number of reasons. These individuals have the choice to let this job loss get to them or pivot and either find a similar job in the same industry or try a new industry altogether. It's possible that you'll pick a job that someday will get overtaken by a robot. Don't worry. Life will go on and you will find another job.

It used to be that you went to college, found a job and stayed at that job for forty years. Today, changing jobs often is becoming the norm. Being a person who can adapt and keep on going is critical to surviving in this world. When I played sports as a child, I'd sometimes get the wind knocked out of me. The coaches were tough on me and would say, "Walk it off." It was their instinct to instill the principle of toughness within me. When you encounter a setback at work, such as a robot replacing you, it's important to "walk it off," breathe and keep on going like nothing happened.

I'm in an industry where I am constantly applying for jobs, getting turned down, or hearing nothing after an interview I thought went well. Sometimes I let this get to me, question if I'm any good, but other times I "walk it off" and move on like nothing happened.

The other day I stumbled upon this video on the internet in which a robot was carrying a package. In an effort to test the robot, the inventor would push the robot back, move the package, and do everything possible to deter this robot. Everything this inventor tried failed in stopping the robot from accomplishing its mission.

Developing toughness as an individual is not something that comes easily to everyone. It's a quality we develop as we fail, make mistakes, and experience many trials and tribulations. When I was in middle school, I was living with my mom and sisters at the time. Because my mom was a single parent for part of my life, her ability to take me places whenever I needed was not always possible. I remember getting a job and having to figure out how I would get there each day. Luckily, it was close enough that I could ride my bike there and back. I could have begged and pleaded with my mom to give me a ride, but instead I pulled my bike out of the garage and took care of the situation by myself. It would have been easy to just give up on the job and say I couldn't do it because I didn't have a ride. That would have been a cop out and I'm thankful I didn't let myself do that.

Footnote:

1   "What jobs are being taken over by robots and computers," https://www.computerhope.com/issues/ch001799.htm, (June 21, 2017)

Chapter 13

Tell your story well

"Personal branding is about managing your name – even if you don't own a business – in a world of misinformation, disinformation, and semi-permanent Google records. Going on a date? Chances are that your 'blind' date has Googled your name.
Going to a job interview? Ditto."

-Tim Ferriss

When you think about soda, you might think about Coca Cola, or Coke. Coke has one of the strongest brands, so much so that soda and Coke are almost interchangeable in some states. There is a word association that is taking place there. Whenever you decide to pick a career, it's important to begin branding yourself from an early age. You don't need to get a tattoo or anything, but getting a business card, creating a website, and maintaining social media profiles such as LinkedIn and Facebook can prove to be beneficial later on.

Today, I brand myself as a "Fixer." Last year, I flew out to three different films that had just lost their first assistant director on their set due to medical leave or personal reasons. I was called in as someone who could come in and essentially "fix" the film set without much prep. I kept thinking about this idea of being a fixer and soon

Tell Your Story Well

decided to create a website: www.thefilmfixer.us. The idea behind the website was instead of buying my name .com, which I had at one point, I could brand myself in a way that people would associate me with someone who could come in and fix a film. I took this even further and developed a business card that lists me as The Film Fixer. Yes, I'm a producer. Yes, I'm a first assistant director. What I wanted people to know is that I can come into any situation and change things around.

One of the most famous branded personalities of all time is Steve Irwin the "Crocodile Hunter." You didn't associate Steve as anything other than the world-famous crocodile hunter. This brand was genius and it's what made him successful.

Now, I'm not recommending that you need to be famous for what you do or that you take it to the extreme like Steve did. The main idea is to brand yourself in way that tells your story over time — what you do and what you are good at.

You don't have to post on Facebook or Instagram everyday what you are doing at work, although an occasional post can't hurt. What you can do is every time there is a WIN in your career, be sure to post an update and be sure to let people know you are winning.

The other day I got a letter in the mail. It was my acceptance into the Producers Guild of America. I was genuinely excited, so I took a picture and posted it to Instagram. From that one picture I got several calls and emails from people who wanted to work with me. Why is that? People saw that I was winning in my career and they wanted to work with a winner.

How you choose to brand yourself is up to you. I'm careful not to put too many crazy or funny pictures on Facebook because I know employers will be looking at this to evaluate whether or not they should hire me.

I make an effort to post mainly pictures, stories, and links that have to do with my career and work. There is nothing wrong with posting pictures or stories of life or you having fun. I simply choose to keep my brand consistent and to post stuff that is in line with what I am doing.

Branding can make or break a career. An employer's first impression is critical to how well you will or will not be received.

Some of the best brands know when it's time to make updates. Around 2010, Jack in the Box made a change to its logo. It was a big thing because this company had held on to its original logo for a very long time. The old logo had the words "Jack in the Box" all in a red box. It wasn't a bad logo, it just felt outdated. In an effort to reach a younger demographic, the company decided to change the logo so that Jack was the only word in the box. It was almost like they were doing a play on words by putting Jack literally in the box. They also updated the box to be three dimensional in nature. I personally love the new logo and think it's smart. The change was needed and will probably last them several decades. This is not to say that you need a logo for yourself, although it couldn't hurt if you have a business card or website. If you know you're not a natural graphic designer, I would recommend paying for a logo. I've paid as little as five dollars on fiverr.com, and as much as several hundred by hiring a professional graphic artist.

Another way people brand themselves is through their communication methods. Every email you send is a brand message about you. The length, the tone, the use of grammar and punctuation, and the email signature itself are all a part of branding. Learning how to send concise, professional emails that have a great email signature can put you a long way ahead of the rest. Personally,

I prefer that people include their phone number in their email signatures. Whenever it's not there, I find it difficult to get in touch with that person because I might want to text or call them instead of sending a long email back. If you aren't sure what a great email signature looks like, Google "best email signature examples." I've done this search many times and each time I am inspired by the various types of signatures. I used to have a complicated signature with a logo, but today I've scaled back to having a more simplistic one with links and my phone number. When I send emails, I make an effort to think about how my tone will come across to the person getting the email. Even adding something at the top of your email such as, "I hope your day is going great," or, "I had a great time meeting you at the party," could go a long way. The main thing to remember is to take your time when sending emails to people you don't regularly speak to in hopes of leaving the best possible impression on them.

Branding can be lots of things. It can be the way you dress, how well you keep your car, and whether or not you follow up. I once interviewed a guy for a position that required lots of attention to detail and organizational know-how. One of the candidates came in raggedly dressed, and even though his resume was decent, I wasn't so sure about him. I walked this person out to his car and could tell he hadn't washed it in six months and there was trash inside. He left a bad impression on me and I decided to hire someone else. Even though he had lots of experience, I wanted to hire someone who would represent my company professionally and I was worried that if he couldn't take care of himself or his car, he wouldn't be able to take care of the many things I needed help with at work.

Branding yourself can be a complicated thing, but let's list a few outlets:

1. Social media (Facebook & LinkedIn)
2. Personal website
3. Business cards
4. Email signature & Email address
5. Resume

Chapter 14

Keep the future in mind

"There's a reason the windshield is bigger than the rearview mirror. Your future matters more than your past!

–Max Lucado

When people talk about careers and jobs, they will often ask what your end goal is. They want to know where you see yourself in your 40s and 50s. Hopefully, in twenty years you will be successful in your career and doing what you've dreamed of. Hopefully, you will have mastered every position in your path and be in a situation where you are now mentoring others in that specific career space. The end goal can be a frightening thing to think about. What if you never make it there?

I know that producing is ultimately my end goal. The path to producing is different for everyone. For me, it was getting a degree in film, working as a production assistant, working as an assistant director and then working as a line producer. Some people just start out producing because they have the money to do so, however, they don't necessarily know what they are doing. These "producers" haven't been in the trenches like I have. I tried not to skip any steps along the way and I made sure I experienced the hard work of virtually every position.

Imagine you wanted to be the owner of a restaurant and were handed one million dollars. You buy the restaurant and things don't seem to be going well. You don't know what's wrong because you've never worked in a restaurant before. Most restaurant owners have a long history of working various restaurant positions. They take this experience with them when they become an owner, and when the busboys are going too slow, the owner can step in and show them how to speed things up.

Imagine you have an ambitious goal to be a senator. How do you get there? What is the path or prior positions that might be helpful before reaching this position? Upon researching the internet[1], it was apparent that to become a senator, it is strongly advised that you should do the following:

1. Get established in the community by running for smaller offices such as city council or the town mayor.
2. Obtain a Bachelor's degree or higher in law, political science and/or business.
3. Have a Party Backing
4. File Candidacy
5. Run a Campaign

What's great about the internet is that you can do this for practically any career out there. Just Google, "How do you become a _____?"

Another way to find this out is by contacting someone in that career field and asking them what steps, prior positions or education they would recommend to work in their industry.

Some people honestly don't know where they want to end up, and that's okay. Sometimes, until you have

Keep The Future In Mind

found the right career and explored all the possible jobs within that career field, it's hard to know where you should end up. As soon as you do figure out where you want to end up, create a goal and write this down on an index card. Maybe place it somewhere on your desk to remind yourself of this audacious vision of yours. The main thing to consider when creating any goal is to understand that the difference between having a goal and writing it down is significant. Writing goals down will help you visualize your future and will be the first of many things that will give your goal legs. Finding people who can hold you accountable to this goal can be a useful practice as well. I find that sharing my dreams with my family and friends is a great way to put that goal out there. I want others to know where I want to go so they can encourage me along the way and offer support. When you start speaking your goal to others, the motivation to move forward will slowly come or increase. I once heard a successful person say it's important to tell the people at the top of the ladder of your career field what you really want to do if you're not currently doing that thing. On many occasions I have told directors and producers that I really want to produce more. While I don't have a ton of requests from people wanting me to take over projects, these people in positions of power do know my interests, and when the time comes, I hope they will consider me for such a task. Sometimes telling others what you really want to do can feel like bragging or being egotistical. It's not. Telling others what you really want to do is inviting them into that space of networking where this guy has a friend of a friend who might need a guy with your skill set. Most of the jobs I get are from situations exactly like that. I rarely get jobs from applying online or sending my resume to a company. I get jobs because people say I'm good at what I do and they vouch for me.

When it comes to understanding the path of where you want to go, it is important to realize that everyone gets to their ideal career high point in different ways. Sure, there might be recommended jobs or career markers you should strive for, but the idea that if you just do this or if you just get a degree you'll be okay is a dangerous one to believe. I bet if you ask ten people in the same career how they ended up there, you would get ten slightly different stories. Of course there would be similarities, but everyone has their own journey, and so will you. There will be times when it might be tempting to do exactly what a certain successful person has done to get where he/she is. Don't fall into this trap. Be okay with paving your own path and blazing your own trail. Don't just read this book on careers, read a few others. Don't just consider one path, consider a few routes to the top.

Sometimes the path to a certain job or career is not always as clear as day. I know many people who built apps, started companies, or decided to be an actor for a living who all had very messy paths. All of these people took huge risks knowing there was an uncertain future ahead of them. Anytime you choose a career with a lot of unknowns, that path is just a little more difficult to define. When this happens, the best thing to do is to give yourself micro-goals. I like to use the phrase "move the needle" because it's an easy analogy for what needs to be done. You essentially want to do small things every day or week that get you to the finish line. This could mean updating your resume, applying for more jobs, or learning a new skill. You want to constantly be evolving and growing as someone who is in position to succeed.

As a film producer, I'm constantly reading scripts, taking meetings, sending emails, and building business plans. For me, the work never stops and there is always an endless amount of things I can do to "move the needle". It's like that movie *What About Bob?* — you have to take baby steps.

Footnote:

1. Caylee Pugh, "So you want to become a senator," https://borgenproject.org/so-you-want-to-become-a-senator/, (August 10, 2016).

Chapter 15

Does my personality matter?

"People accuse me of being arrogant all the time. I'm not arrogant, I'm focused."

-Russell Crowe (INTJ personality)

In school, you spend what feels like an endless amount of time learning terms, equations, and languages in order to master specific subjects. You often have homework, quizzes, and exams to make sure you know, without a doubt, the material your teacher is trying to present to you. All these efforts are focused on the singular goal of learning. It's funny how learning about subjects is given so much weight and yet when it comes to learning about ourselves we take it rather lightly. I think it would be beneficial if high schools or colleges offered an elective course that focused on self-discovery.

Whether or not you have taken a career or personality test at school, it's a good idea to take several of these in high school and college. Taking the same personality test years apart can be helpful because sometimes your growth as a person changes over time, including your likes, dislikes, and how you relate to others in general. There are many personality tests available online and in some schools or churches. I took the Meyers-Briggs Type Indicator test many years ago and found I was an

INTJ. INTJ stands for Introversion, Intuition, Thinking, and Judgment.

According to Myers-Briggs[1], the INTJ have original minds and great drive for implementing their ideas and achieving their goals. Quickly see patterns in external events and develop long-range explanatory perspectives. When committed, organize a job and carry it through. Skeptical and independent, have high standards of competence and performance - for themselves and others.

What I like about this test is the accuracy it provides in learning about YOU. Google the four-letter profiles and learn what types of jobs that specific profile typically has.

I looked at a website[2] that listed common careers for INTJ and found one that I thought was amusing.

Realistic Careers:

- Computer science, systems analyst, informatics, programmer
- Software design
- Engineering (all types)
- Urban planning
- Chemist, mathematician, astronomer, physicist
- Applied science, technology, technician
- Environmental science, geography, geology
- Architect

I wanted to be an architect when I was ten.

Investigative Careers:

- Actuary
- Biochemistry, biology, neuroscience
- Law, lawyer, attorney
- Economics / economist
- Financial planning/planner
- Philosopher, theology, theologian

  In college, I minored in philosophy and worked at a church. You could say I had a little bit of philosopher or theologian in me.

- Health/medical sciences, public health
- Scholar/Researcher
- Social sciences (psychology, sociology, political science, history, anthropology)
- Information / library sciences, librarian

  In high school and college, I was an avid reader and would often read books in place of hanging out with friends.

- Critic, critical theory
- Non-fiction writer

  I'm currently writing this non-fiction book.

- Physician, doctor: neurologist, pathologist, internal medicine

Artistic Careers:

- Graphic/website designer

  I have designed over 50 websites since high school.

- Journalist, editor, blogger

  I was the newspaper editor in high school. I currently have a blog: www.assistantdirecting.com

- Film producer/director

  I'm currently a member of the Producers Guild of America and have produced several movies.

It's possible that the Meyers-Briggs Type Indicator test results don't match up perfectly for you and your future career is not in your personality profile. Taking the Meyers-Brigg is just one of many things to consider when looking at careers options. Remember, you don't want to get in the middle of a career field and realize that you actually hate what you are doing.

To take the test yourself simply visit https://www.mbtionline.com

Footnote:

1. "The 16 MBTI Types," http://www.myersbriggs.org/my-mbti-personality-type/mbti-basics/the-16-mbti-types.htm?bhcp=1

2. Dr. A.J. Drenth, "INTJ Careers, Jobs, & Majors," https://personalityjunkie.com/intj-careers-jobs-majors-part-i/

Chapter 16

Discover by example

"I find that you learn from others. It's very much about watching TV and watching movies for me and grasping that way and watching other people act."

-Callan McAuliffe

Have you ever watched an episode of *Undercover Boss*? If not, I highly recommend you watch every single episode if you want a glimpse into a variety of careers and jobs out there in the marketplace. What's great about *Undercover Boss* is you see the CEO do the ordinary jobs of his employees. You soon realize that some of these jobs are not for you simply by watching this CEO fail time and time again. It's amazing what you can learn about jobs and careers by watching an episode of TV. *Undercover Boss* is not the only show out there that focuses on jobs — there are countless documentaries, reality shows, and even movies that reveal what it's like to work a particular job.

Let's say you are thinking about a career in the medical field. While you can easily binge watch the many TV dramas that focus on hospitals or medicine, you may benefit more from finding a unique documentary or reality show that follows the day in the life of a doctor, surgeon, or nurse. Simply do a search for "medical documentary" on Netflix, Amazon, iTunes, Hulu, or Google. When you find the documentary or TV show, be sure to pay attention and see if that is the type of environment or work you can see yourself doing or that interests you.

When I was in college, I made an effort to watch as many movies as I could. For me, watching movies was research because I wanted to be as well-researched as possible in film. The great thing about watching films is that it's the kind of research that is fun. There aren't that many documentaries about producers or assistant directors, however, I always make an effort to watch the behind the scenes when I purchase a DVD.

While documentaries aren't always the most entertaining, they can prove to be helpful in many instances.

In addition to watching docs and reality shows, another source to consider is YouTube. The list of videos on YouTube on practically any field is mind-blowing. Just begin searching and you will be surprised at the amount of videos you will find.

Podcasts are another great resource to learn about a certain career. I often stream podcasts while I'm working out or on a long drive. I'm always amazed at the wealth of knowledge one can find if you discover just the right channel.

THE CAREER CHOSE ME

Check out this helpful list[1] of Reality TV shows and Documentaries that pertain to various jobs and careers.

REALITY TV

The Job
This series gives candidates from around the country a chance to win positions at some of America's most prestigious companies.

The Apprentice
Contestants compete for a job as an apprentice to billionaire Donald Trump.

Dirty Jobs
Host Mike Rowe takes a look at different dirty jobs with a hands-on approach. The show tackles everything from pigeon feces removal to household clean up after a sewer back up.

Undercover Boss
Bosses of chain businesses go undercover to their own stores in various locations and various jobs around the store and interact with the employees.

America's Toughest Jobs
Contestants are pit against each other as they attempt a series of difficult and dangerous jobs. The prize is the sum of the salaries that would be earned by people doing these jobs in their first year.

DOCUMENTARIES

Steve Jobs: One Last Thing
The visionary co-founder of Apple did things his own way. Jobs, who was obsessed with product details and marketing, has been credited with transforming Apple and changing several industries, including technology, retail, and entertainment. He was also a driven and sometimes ruthless manager. The 2011 PBS documentary will give you a glimpse into Jobs's talent, management style, and imagination, and teach you how marketing is as important as the product you're selling.

One Week Job
Still have no idea what you want to do with your life? After graduating from college, Sean Aiken struggled with that exact question, so he decided to work 52 jobs in 52 weeks to determine his passion. The 2010 documentary follows him as he explores professions ranging from Hollywood producer and stock trader to NHL mascot and real estate agent. To get closer to answering the question, "What do I want to do with my life?" Aiken asks himself and his employers about the nature of success and the real meaning of happiness.

Iris
Albert Maysles's documentary about the life of 95-year-old fashion icon Iris Apfel is a story about the power of creativity. Apfel, who worked on interior and restoration design projects for nine presidents in the White House, built her empire by following her own quirky style and breaking rules along the way. Despite her great success, the quick-witted icon continues to value hard work, which she says is her fountain of youth. "There's always a way,"

Apfel tells CNBC. "There is always a way for anything. Period. If you want something badly enough and you work hard at it, you achieve it. I absolutely guarantee it."

iro Dreams of Sushi
The 2011 documentary profiles Jiro Ono, the first sushi chef to receive three Michelin stars. Japan has called him a national treasure, and yet the 91-year-old master says he still has room to improve: "Even at my age, in my work I haven't reached perfection. I'll continue to climb, trying to reach the top, but no one knows where the top is!" The documentary reveals how dedication and hard work can pay off.

Somm
If you're looking to turn your passion into a career, this documentary will inspire you. *Somm* follows a group of four men attempting to pass the notoriously difficult master sommelier, or wine steward, exam– a test with one of the lowest pass rates in the world. You'll also get a glimpse into the particulars of wine production and consumption around the world.

Don't Look Down
There's rarely a dull moment with Richard Branson. This 2016 documentary tells the story behind the billionaire's attempt to break world records crossing the Atlantic and Pacific in a hot air balloon. "These epic adventures and brushes with death have shaped me to become the person I am today — in fact, they have been pivotal to my success in life; teaching me so many valuable skills and lessons, which I have applied to both business and everyday life," the entrepreneur writes on his blog.

Broke

Part of ESPN's *30 for 30* series, this 2012 documentary reveals how professional athletes have gone from rags to riches and back again in only a few years. Their stories teach an important lesson about lifestyle inflation — and although *Broke* focuses on high-profile athletes, it makes clear that anyone is susceptible to financial ruin.

Footnote:
[1] Kathleen Elkins, "8 documentaries to watch to help further your career," https://www.cnbc.com/2017/01/13/8-documentaries-to-watch-to-help-further-your-career.html, (Jan 13, 2017).

Chapter 17

Volunteer

"We make a living by what we get, but we make a life by what we give."

-Winston Churchill

As a teenager, I had a lot of free time. Time to watch too much TV and hang out with friends. Sure, I had homework and other responsibilities, but I was never burdened with the numerous adult-like responsibilities my parents were often consumed by. When you are young, you naturally have less responsibilities, which means more time to spend doing almost whatever you please. In high school, I kept myself pretty busy by choosing to have a part-time job, spending extra time at school as the newspaper editor, and volunteering at my church in the youth group where I did all things media. These three arenas kept me pretty busy, and volunteering was one of those things that allowed me to really explore and grow in my knowledge of film and media. By being a volunteer I was given a chance to make a difference and utilize my skills and expertise for a cause that was helping others. This got me excited, and those years of volunteering allowed me many opportunities to learn and grow in my skill and knowledge as a filmmaker and as a leader. Part of learning is failing, and as a volunteer

Volunteer

I failed multiple times. I often used my youth group as the test subject when making my first websites. The sites I designed back then weren't anything special, but I was able to build a portfolio in the process. I failed on many occasions when trying to make videos in high school and college. The sound might have been too low or the acting was bad. It was hard because I wanted everything to be perfect and amazing from the start. What I realized was that to get really good at something, you have to do a lot of that thing, and volunteering allowed me an opportunity unlike anything else. Not all my videos were horrible or failures, but some of them were, and I was thankful to have an outlet to fail consistently so that I could slowly get better and learn from my mistakes. After college, I worked at a church in Houston, TX as a video producer. I periodically had teenagers come into the office and volunteer their time like I once did. They would write scripts, shoot and edit videos, and act in various projects. The tables had turned and now I was the one with the job and I was able to recruit teenagers to volunteer to assist me in the projects I was creating. I went from being the volunteer to recruiting and managing volunteers in my twenties. This was a great opportunity for many of my volunteers because some of those students were interested in acting or going into the film industry. Just like me, those students "got" the importance of volunteering their time. Being involved provided an opportunity to volunteer where there was a need and this gave them an opportunity to learn at the same time. Like me, maybe some of their volunteer time will pay off in the end.

 Over the years I have spent countless hours volunteering. I can't say that every time I volunteered I learned something, but I can say that volunteering overall has helped me to grow as a leader and become a better person. I've been on multiple trips across the world (Russia, Africa,

Honduras, Mexico) and have helped people in third world countries who are less privileged than most of us. I was fortunate because on almost all of these trips I was the one in charge, documenting the trip's efforts with my video camera. I felt blessed because I was getting an opportunity to volunteer and still use my gifts and passions for film. Without me being there to document these trips, it's possible the story of our efforts would go untold. Every time I came back from one of these trips I had this enormous feeling of gratitude that was almost indescribable. Those trips changed me as a person for the better as I was becoming a person who understood the world's problems.

If you are ever feeling ungrateful, just spend a few days building a house with Habitat for Humanity. You don't have to be skilled, just willing to lift a hammer. If you ever feel that you don't own as many clothes as you think you deserve, then try spending a day sorting recycled clothes at the local Goodwill or homeless shelter. If you ever feel that you don't have as many things as you wish you could own, consider going on a trip overseas where you can serve a third world country or even consider buying gifts for underprivileged kids this Christmas by participating in a toy drive.

Every sector of life uses volunteers in one way or another. The list of organizations that continually need volunteers is essentially endless. Volunteering not only helps your community, it helps you. When you volunteer your time and energy into a cause or organization you care about, you are essentially exchanging your time for personal and professional growth. Even if the volunteer assignment is as simple as helping in a homeless shelter or food bank, you will benefit as you slowly become a person who helps the less fortunate.

Volunteer

There are also many opportunities to volunteer for organizations, churches, and institutions such as hospitals that will give you a glimpse into specific careers.

If working with animals is something that interests you, then volunteering at a local animal shelter could give you a firsthand experience that would help determine your level of interest down the road.

If you like the idea of working in the medical field, there are many opportunities to volunteer in hospitals – like visiting kids with cancer.

Let's say you want to run for office someday. There are opportunities to volunteer at political rallies. You can also find a candidate you support and see how you can volunteer to help with his/her campaign.

For every career there are endless opportunities to give your time and help a cause. You will learn and the organization will benefit from your contribution. Not sure where to start? Do some research on the internet and send a few emails. A lot of times volunteer opportunities aren't listed–you will just need to ask.

Chapter 18

Don't be cool

"You think you're too cool for school, but I have a newsflash for you, Walter Cronkite...you aren't."

-Derek Zoolander (Zoolander)

Growing up, I was never what you would consider to be a "cool kid." I didn't sit at the "cool" lunch table. I didn't play "cool sports" like football. I didn't always dress "cool" or have all the "cool" friends. I guess you could say I was destined to be uncool the rest of my life. It's funny looking back on this concept of "cool," because what I have discovered in my industry today is that it doesn't matter at all how "cool" you were growing up. No one cares. No one is quizzing me about what lunch table I sat at in junior high or if I played on the varsity football team in high school. The only thing people care about when they are evaluating me to possibly work for their company is my work experience, education, and ability get things done.

Many of my old classmates think I have a "cool" job since I work in the film/TV industry as a producer and assistant director. Having a certain job doesn't necessarily make you cool, but it can have benefits and fun bragging rights on occasion. I don't always feel "cool" at work, but whenever I walk the red carpet at a film festival or

Don't Be Cool

premiere for a film I worked, then I feel cool, and that definitely feels good.

May I suggest that you don't pick a career based on its "cool factor." Sure, it will be fun to tell your friends or family that you want to be an astronaut or a movie star, but is that desire to be "cool" really worth it? A very small percentage of astronauts ever make it to space, and I personally only know a handful of actors who can even consider themselves to be working actors.

When you are picking a career, pick something based on your passions, skills, and genuine interests. As tempting as it is to pick something that will sound "cool" to others, don't fall into this trap. After you leave high school or college, the chance that you will hang out with the same friends is actually quite low. Either you or your friends will move away and you will find new friends who will most likely work in the same industry. You don't want to get involved in a career so you can prove to your friends that you "made it." Decide to be an adult at fourteen and pick a career based on what makes you YOU.

Hanging out with my friends in school, we would talk about our futures and what we were going to do for a living. We would discuss college majors and future career aspirations. It was often embarrassing if you didn't have a plan or didn't know exactly what you wanted to do. The thing to remember is that these conversations will come and go but your career will last you a lifetime.

As tempting as it is to tell everyone that you want to be a doctor or lawyer, take a long, hard look at those careers and really ask yourself if that is the type of work you want to do for 50 years or more.

It's possible that you are a guy and want to be a nurse. While this is a predominately female profession, don't let that get you down. The number of male nurses is increasing. It would be a shame if this person decided to NOT be a nurse based on their friends or family buying into this stereotype and were afraid he would become uncool.

You may believe that you are above being "cool" and you have it figured out. Believe me, I thought I was above it too. For the longest time I wanted to be a director of photography because, to me, this was the coolest job in the film industry. I spent years learning about cameras, working as a first assistant camera, and camera operator. When I first moved to Los Angeles, I worked on several movies in the camera department and even flew to New York to shoot a documentary as a camera operator. Through these experiences I learned that while I enjoyed this somewhat, a large part of my reasoning for wanting to do such a thing was not based on my natural skills or abilities. Sure, I was learning and getting better, but a lot of the technical things DPs know and understand didn't come easy to me. What came easy to me was logistics, schedules, and management. Why did I waste all this time and energy attempting to do something that didn't come naturally to me? Well, to be honest, I wanted to be "cool" and wanted others to think I was "cool." I thought this idea of "cool" from junior high hadn't fazed me, but it was sticking with me that whole time. I wanted to be the one in the behind the scenes photograph operating the camera. I wanted to be in on the action and up close with the director. Once I realized that having this "cool" job wasn't all it was cracked up to be, I switched gears and began working in jobs that I was naturally good at. I found myself producing and working as an assistant director and loving it. These were the types of jobs that came easy to me and jobs I knew I could excel at quickly.

Chapter 19

There are no Lone Rangers

"Every successful individual knows that his or her achievement depends on a community of persons working together."

-Paul Ryan

As human beings, we tend to gravitate towards doing things with others. It's not "normal" to live, play, and work alone. It's funny how even something as simple as going to the movies with another person is more fun than going by yourself. Even though you won't interact with that person during the movie, just knowing you are not alone in a dark theater is somehow comforting.

When it comes to work and careers, a majority of jobs are ones in which you will interact with others, have coworkers or depend on certain relationships to get things done. Your ability to build and maintain these relationships could be critical to having a successful career and could even benefit your overall wellbeing.

As you begin to get excited or passionate about a certain career, make an effort to find people who have similar passions or interests and get to know them. Join a club, organization, or sports team– something where you can find people with the same interests.

THE CAREER CHOSE ME

One of the great things about attending college is finding lots of people with similar career ambitions when you start to take classes in your specific major. When I was in college, it was so cool that there were literally hundreds of people there who wanted to do exactly what I wanted to do for a living. Befriend those people and make it a point to hang out with them and pick their brains. Perhaps you can ask them why they want to major in this or work as that. Maybe your friend with a similar career ambition will give you ideas of how to move forward and what they personally have learned along their journey. No one wants to figure out this career thing by themselves, and by having a trusted confidante, you will make your life easier. I can remember wondering how I would get to know some of these people since we didn't seem to talk much in class. It wasn't until later in college when I started doing group projects that I got to know more and more people in my major. Group projects made it easier to build friendships because we were spending time outside of class strategizing about the assignment. In addition to these group projects I slowly figured out that the more things I could do outside of class with my classmates, the better. There is value in creating meaningful projects with people you enjoy being around.

In college, I had several friends and roommates who all had similar passions to make films. I can remember having deep, meaningful conversations about film with them. We would discuss film theory, film auteurs and just geek out over the latest movies that were playing at the theaters. I think this camaraderie was helpful in forming my taste of what I liked and what I found to be artful.

There is something to be said about having a close friend who wants to do the same thing you do. When you get older, most of your friends will be people from work or people who work in the same industry.

There Are No Lone Rangers

In addition to friends and colleagues, I have found it extremely helpful to speak with seasoned professionals who have been there and done that. Perhaps you can find a mentor in the field you are interested in who can guide you. A lot of times these mentorships will look like glorified internships.

When I first moved to Los Angeles, I made it a point to learn as much as I could as quickly as I could. I interned with three different production companies, and at each company I learned new things that I would have never learned in college. The thing about internships is they often don't pay and the tasks are repetitive and boring. You have to really humble yourself. But it will be worth it in the long run. During these internships I was able to get an in-depth look at how film development works. I got to do things like give notes on screenplays, build social media marketing campaigns, and even assist in building websites. Everything I learned through those internships proved to be invaluable as I grew in my career.

Another thing to consider when trying to connect with others and grow in your knowledge is to seek advice from the pros. This can look and feel different in a variety of ways. I once reached out to an assistant director who worked on *Prison Break*. I didn't personally know this person but I knew someone she had worked with and this was enough to get a meeting with her. We grabbed coffee and I got to ask her about her experiences in the film industry. Since that meeting I haven't worked with her, but I have stayed in contact on Facebook and occasionally see her at industry functions. I've probably had a dozen of these types of meetings over the years. Sometimes I am the one seeking advice and guidance, and other times people are wanting to meet with me to pick my brain. Even though these meetings are often one-time meetings, a lot of times there is huge value in them and I make an effort to be proactive and schedule these meetings or they may never happen.

People hire people they know– the saying is very true. If I have the option to hire someone I know and trust over hiring someone based off a resume, I can guarantee that the person I know will be first in line. If you truly know and understand this principle, your view of networking will change. Networking is more than just grabbing someone's business card at a conference. To me, networking is all about continuing relationships with people I work with. Whenever I find people I enjoy working with, I make sure to find them on social media, add them as a friend, and stay in touch with them.

Sometimes just reminding people that you exist is all you need to do in order to land a job. I frequently attend workshops and conferences in my field and run into people I know. I make sure to say hi, make small talk and see what they are up to. I try not to sell myself too much, but if the opportunity exists, I tell them what I'm up to, give them my card and do a soft pitch. It's funny how many jobs have come from just reaching out to old work colleagues who didn't know I was looking for work. While this type of approach applies mainly to careers like mine that are freelance, almost any industry will show preference to an existing relationship.

Chapter 20

Don't be afraid of the unknown

"Land is the secure ground of home, the sea is like life, the outside, the unknown."

-Stephen Gardiner

In college, I was majoring in film but not really sure what exact job title I would have after I graduated. I knew I was interested in cinematography and I knew I enjoyed producing, but I didn't really know what it meant to be a director of photography or a producer.

After years of wearing many hats and trying many positions on countless film sets, I finally figured out what the best "job" for me was. I figured out that being an assistant director and line producer were two jobs that really fit me well. It wasn't really until I turned thirty that I was able to discover these jobs. For some, this may sound like I was late to discover this, however, I know many people who live their entire lives and never find that perfect "job" that matches up with their interests, passions, and skills. Part of the discovery for me was trying lots of different things in the film sector. I worked as an editor, writer, director, cinematographer, producer...essentially, I did a little bit of everything and figured out my strengths and weaknesses. I realized that although I enjoyed being behind the camera, I didn't enjoy the decision-making

THE CAREER CHOSE ME

process that was required when I wore the hat of director of photography. When I was presented with an opportunity to write scripts, I learned that while I enjoyed writing, the idea of being a full-time writer was scary to me. I worked on a film set in the capacity of a camera assistant many times, and while it was an exciting job, I honestly wasn't that good at pulling focus.

All these experiences led me to one day find myself as the first assistant director on a film set. I remember it like it was yesterday because I had to pinch myself to believe I was really getting paid to do it. The other jobs I had experienced had their benefits, but this particular job got me up in the morning. If you are unfamiliar with what the role of the first assistant director is, it's basically the person who manages a film crew of a movie set. As a first assistant director I create the entire schedule for a film, coordinate all logistics with each department, set the extras and work with the director to keep track of time and make the day.

When I began doing this job, there was something within me that came alive. It was like hearing that voice within me that said, "This is what YOU were made to do." This job not only matched with my natural skill set as a leader, it was something that I became quite good at quickly. Since my time working as a first AD, I've worked on dozens of movies, coordinated police car chases, stunts and worked with esteemed crew members such as Dean Cundey (director of photography for *Jurassic Park* and *Back to the Future*).

I could have been a first AD when I was in film school, but I didn't think the job was for me. I made the mistake of not exploring. Sometimes I kick myself for not discovering this job earlier, but then I have to give myself a break and be thankful for finding it when I did.

As you think about your future career and your future "perfect job," it's a good thing to be open to many

Don't Be Afraid Of The Unknown

possibilities. Try out as many positions and jobs within the career you are pursuing until you land the one that gets you fired up. It's okay to try jobs that you find you aren't really that good at. When you do find that job that isn't for you, cross it off your list and move on to the next one.

Let's say you want a career doing something with computers. Where do you start? Maybe you start by taking computer science classes or looking online. You end up taking ten different courses but one course is about web design. For some reason, you enjoy this course more than anything else. It's not a giveaway, but maybe you should explore working as a web designer. Build a few sites, find a webmaster mentor, and see how you enjoy it. If it's something you enjoy, then talk with someone in the field and ask them what types of positions there are in the web design field.

Here are a few examples of careers as a web designer:

1. Web graphic designer
2. Web designer
3. Multimedia / Web designer
4. User interface designer

While some of these positions or "jobs" are similar, they all have their differences and flavors that make them unique. Some of these jobs require college degrees and some just a great eye for design.

If you just decided you want to be a webmaster without doing the proper research, you might fail to realize that there are actually many different careers and career paths within the umbrella of creating websites.

Over the years, I have developed dozens of websites. Sometimes I have done everything from the design and programming, and sometimes I have served as the project manager where I had a team of designers and programmers under me. The best websites always came when I worked as a team and relied on people who were experts in their field to do their specific tasks.

Chapter 21

Say NO to things

"It's only by saying no that you can concentrate on the things that are really important."

-Steve Jobs

This is a tough one. I love to say yes. I hate letting people down, but sometimes you have to say no to things and people and opportunities. By saying no to certain things, you are allowing yourself to say yes to the right things.

Several years ago, I was in the middle of breaking into the film industry in Los Angeles and all of a sudden I landed a job that had nothing to do with film. The company sold luxury products and I had helped them build their website and produce a few videos. They wanted me to work for their company full-time and really help their start-up get to the top. It was exciting to feel wanted and needed. I liked the idea of having a full-time job because I didn't have many prospects for work at that time. It was an easy answer for me because I quickly said NO. I knew that by saying NO to this wonderful opportunity that had nothing to do with my career, I was saying YES to possible opportunities in the future. When you are working full-time for a company, you can't easily take off to go work on projects as you please, or at least I thought I couldn't. What's funny is that the moment I said NO, the company made the offer that I could work for them in between my film projects. I was astounded—it sounded too good to be true. In the end, I worked for this company for a year, and was grateful for the opportunity to have the flexibility I needed to break into my industry.

There will be many cool things that come your way. People will want to hang out with you, companies will want to hire you and you will be asked to do many, many things. The question you have to ask yourself is if a person or experience will benefit your career in the future. If the job, opportunity or person will not benefit your future or career, then make sure to stop and think before instantly saying YES.

Over the years, I've turned down many opportunities to hang out with friends, attend parties or accept certain jobs because the choices didn't align with where I wanted to go financially or career-wise. Sometimes it was easy, and other times I had FOMO (fear of missing out). I hate the idea of letting people down or missing out on a lucrative opportunity. One thing I have learned is that being laser-focused on what I want to do has made it bearable, knowing that I have a goal and a plan. I don't want to just work in my industry– I want to *thrive*.

Chapter 22

The ultimate test

"Your career is your business. It's time for you to manage it as a CEO."

-*Dorit Sher*

There are many online career tests available that will help you narrow down your search based on your personality and preferences. I would recommend taking a few of these tests. Even if they cost money, it's worth the price. Oftentimes, schools will offer a career test, however, this might not be offered until it's really late in the game, like in your senior year of high school. If you have the option, take a career test when you are in ninth or tenth grade. Taking a test at that time gives you the ability to really think about different careers before you might be forced to declare a major. To find the most current career test, simply Google "best online career test" and you will find a list of online tests to choose from.

Take advantage of these tests, because being honest and spending 30 minutes answering a few questions could really help you discover a career you might or might not have thought about.

Here are a few tests you might check out:

https://www.sokanu.com/
Sokanu has developed the most comprehensive career test ever built. The Sokanu career test is a 20-minute interest, personality, and preference assessment that measures you against over 100 traits and uses that data to accurately match you to over 800 careers.

http://www.self-directed-search.com/
The next generation of John Holland's Self-Directed Search® (SDS®) is a career assessment and exploration tool that matches your aspirations, activities and talents to the career choices and educational opportunities that fit you best.

https://www.mynextmove.org/explore/ip
Sponsored by the US Department of Labor, this tool uses a method similar to Self-Directed Search to help you identify where your career interests lie, then points you towards career paths that might feed those interests.

http://www.myplan.com/
MyPlan.com offers a suite of four different tests to help you find your perfect career and measure your career personality (similar to the MBTI), interests, skills and desired values (the only free test on the site).

https://www.pymetrics.com/
Pymetrics uses a series of simple yet surprisingly challenging mind games to measure different cognitive and social traits—your level of risk aversion or your attention span. The results detail your strengths and weaknesses, which can give you some hints into what kinds of roles you might excel in.

// REVIEW AND REFLECT //

You've made it through the book and now it's time to put pen to paper and really come up with some possible careers. If you are reading this on a Kindle, iPad or other electronic device, consider writing these answers down on a pad of paper or type them on your computer.

Don't feel like you have to decide today what you want to do for the rest of your life. What you can decide is how you want to begin your search for the career that is meant for you. It's easy to read these questions and answer them to yourself. Make an effort to spend a few hours going over these questions, writing your answers down, and doing some research.

- List five careers you wanted to have when you were really little:
  1. _____
  2. _____
  3. _____
  4. _____
  5. _____

- What was it about any of these careers that attracted you to them?

THE CAREER CHOSE ME

- List ten things you are passionate about:
  1. _____
  2. _____
  3. _____
  4. _____
  5. _____
  6. _____
  7. _____
  8. _____
  9. _____
  10. _____

- List five strengths you possess:
  1. _____
  2. _____
  3. _____
  4. _____
  5. _____

- List five possible career options based on your strengths and passions:
  1. _____
  2. _____
  3. _____
  4. _____
  5. _____

- How much money do you want to make when you are older?
  A. $10,000-$30,000 (entry-level income jobs)
  B. $30,000 -$50,000 (middle-income jobs)
  C. $50,000 - $80,000 (upper middle-income jobs)
  D. $80,000 - $100,000 (high-income jobs)
  E. $100,000+ (six-figure income jobs)

The Ultimate Test

- Do any of the careers you currently have in mind line up with the salary you desire?
  A. Yes
  B. No
  C. I'm Not Sure
  D. Possibly

- If the career you are thinking about isn't naturally lucrative, what other ways could you make money that aren't dependent on that specific job?
  1. _____
  2. _____
  3. _____

- List five jobs you have had in the past that required a lot of manual labor:
  1. _____
  2. _____
  3. _____
  4. _____
  5. _____

- Do you tend to enjoy work that uses your mental, creative or physical abilities, or maybe all three?
  A. Mental
  B. Creative
  C. Physical
  D. All of the Above

- What was the first job you ever had?
  _____

- Was this a positive or negative experience?
  A. Positive
  B. Negative

THE CAREER CHOSE ME

- Do you have any ambitions that are RISKY in nature? (Like being a singer or actor.)
  _____

- If so, have you asked for critical feedback from experts?
  A. YES
  B. NO

- Pick a career and then investigate three new jobs within that career you have never heard of.
  CAREER _____
  JOB #1 _____
  JOB #2 _____
  JOB #3 _____

- Find a book on the topic of one of your career paths and read it.

- Schedule a recurring event on your calendar to remind yourself to dedicate time to focus on your future career. Maybe pick a time like every Sunday night at 8 p.m.

- Ask your family and friends about their jobs.

- Are you planning on attending college? List a few of your college choices:
  1. _____
  2. _____
  3. _____

- On the fence about college? Talk to 3-5 people in the career you wish to pursue and get their advice.

Recommended Reading

I highly recommend you read *StrengthsFinder 2.0* by Tom Rath. This book is incredible and insightful when it comes to figuring out your strengths.

They have a test called CliftonStrengths that you can take online.

https://www.gallupstrengthscenter.com

Spread the word

If this book, *The Career Chose Me*, made an impact on you and has truly helped in your decision-making process, please consider taking a few minutes to write a review on Amazon. Reviews don't have to be long, they can be one or two sentences–everything helps!

If someone you know could benefit from this book, maybe they are in high school, college or in a transitional point in their life, consider gifting this book to them as encouragement for them to find their ultimate career.

If you would like to order copies of this book for your school, organization or group of friends, please visit www.thecareerchoseme.com.

Finally, please stay in touch and follow me online. You can write me by sending me an email to brandon@radiantfirst.com or following me online.

facebook.com/radiantfirst
instagram.com/radiantfirst

About the Author

Brandon Riley grew up in the mid-cities area near DFW Texas. With an interest in film and telling stories at an early age, he quickly became the editor of the school newspaper in high school. Brandon obtained a bachelor's degree in radio/TV/film and a minor in philosophy from the University of North Texas. Upon graduation, he moved to Houston, Texas to work at a church as a creative media producer. While working there, he wrote, shot, and edited hundreds of short format videos from script to screen. In 2012, he moved from Houston, Texas to Los Angeles, California with the goal of breaking into the film industry. He started off interning with various production companies, working for free and cheap.

Today, Brandon is making a living as a full-time freelance film professional. He is a member of the Directors Guild of America and the Producers Guild of America. He has worked on more than thirty movies as an assistant director or producer. In his free time, he writes screenplays, blogs, and mentors others in the arena of film.

CPSIA information can be obtained
at www.ICGtesting.com
Printed in the USA
LVHW050424210520
656158LV00018B/2166